Managing People

B

In Charge
Series Editor: Roger Cartwright

Managing People

A COMPETENCE APPROACH TO SUPERVISORY MANAGEMENT

Foreword from the MCI

Roger Cartwright • Michael Collins
George Green • Anita Candy

BLACKWELL
Business

IN CHARGE

Copyright © Roger Cartwright, Michael Collins, George Green and
Anita Candy, 1993, 1998

First published 1993
Revised and updated edition printed 1998

Blackwell Publishers Ltd
108 Cowley Road, Oxford OX4 1JF, UK

Blackwell Publishers Inc
350 Main Street, Malden, Massachusetts 02148, USA

British Library Cataloguing in Publication Data
A CIP catalogue record for this book is available from the British Library

Library of Congress Cataloging in Publication Data
Managing people : a competence approach to supervisory management /
Roger Cartwright ... [et al.]. — Rev. and updated ed.
p.   cm. — (In charge)
"NVQ/SVQ level 3."
Includes bibliographical references and index.
ISBN 0–631–20923–9 (alk. paper)
1. Supervision of employees. I. Cartwright, Roger. II. Series.
HF5549.12.M355   1997   97–45216
658.3'02—dc21   CIP

Typeset in 11.5 on 14pt Palatino
by Joshua Associates Ltd, Oxford and Getset, Eynsham, Oxford
Printed and bound in Great Britain
by Athenæum Press Ltd, Gateshead, Tyne & Wear

This book is printed on acid-free paper

Contents

Managing oneself to optimize results; showing self-confidence and personal drive; managing personal emotions and stress; managing personal learning and development.

List of Figures

Foreword

Improving management performance through better competence-based management development is the key to increasing the performance of individual managers, as well as business organizations, and hence of the economy as a whole.

Successfully used by a wide range of organizations in private, public and not-for-profit sectors throughout the UK, MCI's new, integrated Management Standards are firmly established as the benchmark by which the effectiveness of individual managers may be judged.

In focusing on the supervisory level, this book provides a practical and accessible means of acquiring the knowledge and understanding essential to better performance in the workplace, and to the acquisition of vocational qualifications.

The numerous case notes drawn from the practical experience clearly illustrate those elements of generic supervisory management that are critical to success in most organizations, if completed to the right standards.

I therefore warmly commend this book to all candidates who seek to develop such qualifications, both as far as their own personal development, and achieving their organization's specific objectives, are concerned.

Professor Tom Cannon
Chief Executive
Management Charter Initiative

For June, Yvonne, Bronwen and Philip

We would like to express our grateful thanks to all those who have provided help and criticism during the preparation of the volumes of *In Charge*, especially to Blackwell Publishers and their reviewers – Donna Green of Rover Group, Jane Hawkins of NEBSM Regional Managers, Evelyn Lee-Barber of Bass plc, Sandy Milton of the Radcliffe Infirmary Oxford, and Terry Guy and Debbie Stones of Autotype International.

Jean walked out of the door trying to control her breathing. She hadn't known why Mr Rawlings wanted to see her, although she didn't think that she'd done anything wrong.

When he offered her the vacant position of section supervisor (vacant because Jim had moved to the new offices) on a temporary basis pending the outcome of the current organizational review, she was filled with a mixture of thoughts:

> The money would be useful
>
> What about the responsibility?
>
> What would the staff think?
>
> How much extra time would it take?

She'd asked about Alan and Maureen who were both senior to her, but Mr Rawlings had said that Alan was taking up an offer of early retirement and Maureen wanted a job share that was on offer in another department.

She'd accepted the position but as she walked down the corridor one question above all others kept coming back into her mind:

> 'He's told me I'm going to be *In Charge* . . . but
> what does that actually mean?'

Chapter 1
Introduction

- What the *In Charge* series is about
- Who the series is intended for
- Programmes for which the volumes will be useful
- Scope of the volumes
- How to use the volumes

WHAT THE *IN CHARGE* SERIES IS ABOUT

The three volumes in this series are designed to provide those in supervisory and first line management positions with the knowledge and skills to carry out their supervisory and management tasks with competence.

WHO THE SERIES IS INTENDED FOR

If you have responsibilities for others within your organization or you are seeking such responsibility, you will find this series useful. You may have been in your post for some time, you may have been promoted recently or you may be seeking promotion: in all these cases, this series will provide you with useful knowledge and understanding to support you within the work situation and will aid you with your managerial/supervisory and personal development.

The series is intended to be equally relevant to all areas of work and contains cases from the private, public and voluntary sectors.

The series will also provide useful material for those responsible for training at this level, and has been specially designed to support National Vocational Qualification (NVQ) or Scottish Vocational Qualification (SVQ) programmes at supervisory management level 3.

PROGRAMMES FOR WHICH THE VOLUMES WILL BE USEFUL

In Charge has been written to support supervisory/first line management (FLM) development programmes at NVQ or SVQ level 3 in addition to company short courses and individual development. Such courses, validated by BTEC, ISM and NEBSM, are offered by a large number of further education establishments, and also by open learning providers.

Should you decide to undertake formal supervisory/FLM development, *In Charge* will be of considerable benefit, written as the volumes are by a team whose experience includes both practical management in both the private and public sector, and many years working on and producing management development programmes for supervisors and managers.

SCOPE OF THE VOLUMES

The areas covered are:

Volume 1 *Managing People*

This volume commences by looking at how ideas of supervision and management have developed over time and then considers how to manage people effectively, covering: motivation; human reactions to change; recruitment, selection and training; working with teams and groups; leadership; handling conflict. It concludes with a consideration of the role of the supervisor/FLM in the discipline and grievance process.

Volume 2 *Managing Activities*

This volume looks at the operations of an organization and the part played by supervisors and junior managers. The volume examines the different types of organizations you will encounter – public sector, private sector, etc. – and considers the relationship between operations and other organizational functions, such as marketing and personnel. The volume then examines the operations function in more detail, covering both work practices, planning, resourcing, legislation, etc., and customer relations.

Volume 3 *Managing Resources and Information*

This volume covers two key areas of supervision and first line management. Managing information examines the types of information the supervisor/FLM is likely to encounter, and considers ways of disseminating and presenting such information. The finance section is designed to give the reader a broad overview of the role finance plays in an organization; it is not intended to turn the reader into an accountant, but rather to provide the supervisor/FLM with an understanding of financial language and practices as they relate to the work situation.

Volume 4 *Managing Yourself*

A volume dedicated to personal competence.

HOW TO USE THE VOLUMES

No set of books, however well written, can provide the answer to a specific problem that an individual has encountered. However, by providing the individual with an insight into the processes that are at work within situations, and with opportunities to examine situations from a variety of standpoints, books such as those in the *In Charge* series can allow the supervisor/FLM to make more informed decisions.

How an individual uses these books will depend on the situation they find themselves in, it might be that:

1 You are taking a one-year supervisory management course and have been advised to read chapters 6 and 7 of volume 1 to support your classroom work on teams and leadership. In that case you should consider the material in the light of the lectures and seminars you have attended and use the information in the book to support the taught input.

2 You may be involved in an open learning programme, in which case the books can add to the information contained in your open learning programme.

3 If you are attending a company-based short course, the *In Charge* books will provide you with extra information that can

be used to explore areas that you have developed a special interest in.

4 Perhaps you have been newly appointed into a supervisory/FLM position. *In Charge*, read systematically first and then used as an aid for specific problem areas, will provide you with the knowledge and understanding necessary for your new responsibilities.

5 If you have been in a supervisory/FLM position for some time and you wish to gain further knowledge or you are seeking further promotion, *In Charge* will provide you with the language and concepts necessary to develop.

Use the volumes as you would a handbook: scan through first to gain the flavour of the subject and then you can home in on specifics. The volumes form an integrated package and while each can stand alone, at the same time they support each other and refer you backwards and forwards. Supervision and first line management tasks cannot be pigeon-holed into purely Managing People or solely Managing Finance, and neither can an effective supporting text.

Chapter 2
Being In Charge

- Supervisors and managers – what's in a title?
- Importance of management/supervisory development
- Management/supervisory development programmes

Different organizations provide different job titles for staff holding supervisory and first line management positions, for example:

Supervisor	Foreman
Chargehand	Senior . . . .
First Line Manager	NCO (Armed Forces)
Junior Manager	Assistant Manager
Trainee Manager	Team Leader
Coordinator	Administrator
Section Leader	Staff Nurse

SUPERVISORS AND MANAGERS – WHAT'S IN A TITLE?

Organizations within the United Kingdom display little consistency in the titles given to those working in supervisory/junior management positions. One company may consider a person to be a supervisor while another company may designate a similar post 'assistant manager', it all depends on the type of company, the way in which positions have evolved and industry custom and practice. In chapter 3 of the first volume, *Managing People*, there is an examination of the tasks that managers/supervisors undertake, and you will see that there are no clear-cut distinctions between the tasks undertaken by the various job titles, indeed a supervisor in one organization may have considerably more responsibility than an assistant manager in another. One way of making sense of the distinctions is to consider the degree of decision-making power a person has against their involvement in the 'hands on' part of the tasks of their section, department, etc. This can be seen in figure 2.1.

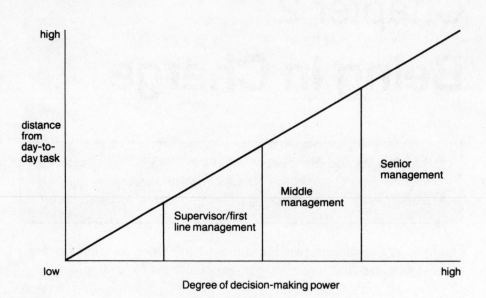

Figure 2.1 The supervisory/management continuum

THINK POINT

- Where does your job fit within the above model?
- How much decision-making power have you got?
- How much do you want?

The model suggests that the difference among the titles is reflected by the degree of decision-making power a person holds and their distance from the core tasks of the organization. Another way of looking at this is to consider the 'focus' a person needs as part of their job.

1 Senior management need to focus on the whole organization.
2 The focus of middle management may be the whole department.
3 The focus of supervisors/junior managers is more likely to be on a part of a department.

It is clear however that there is considerable overlap among these designations and for the purpose of this series the target group can be defined as:

Those who are responsible for a group of employees and/or operations and who have prime responsibility for ensuring the completion of a number of tasks within a section of the organization but need to refer much of the non-routine decision making to their immediate superior.

Let us consider some examples.

Paul is a junior manager within a large store. He has day-to-day responsibility for the hardware department and takes his place on the rota as store duty manager one day per month. Paul has six assistants reporting to him. He needs to refer to the assistant general manager for any major changes he wishes to make to the layout of the department but is able to make decisions relating to staff rotas, refunds etc. in his department within the overall policy of the store.

Andrea is the supervisor in charge of ten machinists in a garment factory. She reports directly to the production manager who informs her of the work required. Andrea then ensures that supplies are available and that the work is scheduled to meet the required deadlines.

Sylvia is the stock administrator in a small pharmaceutical company. Whilst she has no staff reporting to her directly, she is responsible for ensuring that the operations of the company are supplied with the necessary stock and thus has a great deal of liaison work with other departments.

THINK POINT

Think about Paul, Andrea and Sylvia. Do you agree that they all fit the definition of a supervisor/first line manager (FLM) as given earlier?

Sylvia, Andrea and Paul fit our earlier definition although they work in different fields and have different job titles. If you have, or wish for, responsibilities like theirs, this series will help you.

Having a supervisory/FLM title does not mean that all you do is supervise or manage. The degree of supervisory/management tasks will vary from organization to organization and indeed between departments and sections within an organization. Figure 2.2 shows some patterns of supervision showing the degree of supervision carried out.

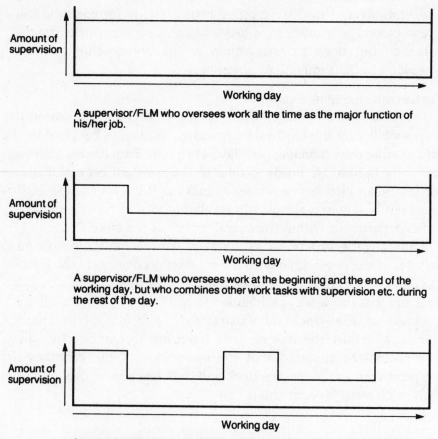

A supervisor/FLM who oversees work all the time as the major function of his/her job.

A supervisor/FLM who oversees work at the beginning and the end of the working day, but who combines other work tasks with supervision etc. during the rest of the day.

A supervisor/FLM who oversees during shift changes and who has other duties in addition during the rest of the working day.

Figure 2.2 The patterns of supervision/first line management

THE IMPORTANCE OF SUPERVISOR/MANAGEMENT DEVELOPMENT

In 1987, Professor Charles Handy produced a report entitled *The Making of Managers* in which he contrasted Management Development in the UK with that undertaken in other EEC countries, the USA and Japan. Some of the findings were dramatic to say the least:

- With 4 times the UK population, the USA provides 40 times more management development experience.
- Only 21 per cent of UK managers have any form of managerial qualification.

- Even when management development is provided by companies, less than 50 per cent of managers participate.
- 90,000 new managers enter the UK economy annually; in 1987 only 10,000 of them obtained training.

With this in mind, the Management Charter Initiative was set up (see chapter 3 of this volume) and given the task of developing competence standards and promoting management development within the UK.

Management Development is not a 'one off' piece of training but an on-going process that an individual partakes of during their career. Management Development encompasses:

1 Nationally recognized qualifications such as: Certificate in Supervisory Management, Certificate in Management (CM/ CMS), Diploma in Management Studies (DMS), Master of Business Administration (MBA). Such courses are validated by a number of bodies: Business and Technology Education Council (BTEC), Open University, Institute of Supervisory Management (ISM), National Examining Board for Supervisory Management (NEBSM), University Business Schools etc. and may, if based on a competence approach, qualify for a National Vocational Qualification (NVQ) or Scottish Vocational Qualification (SVQ) at levels 3–5. A variety of means of obtaining these qualifications exists in the UK comprising both taught and open learning programmes.

The *In Charge* series is designed to support programmes for supervisors/FLMs at NVQ or SVQ level 3.

Many of those who study at this level will wish to progress up the management development ladder, and the underpinning knowledge and understanding gained from the *In Charge* series will be of considerable benefit.

2 In company courses: many companies run short courses for management staff and the *In Charge* series can support such courses. If properly accredited, company courses can form part of a nationally recognized qualification.

3 Individual development: even if there is no opportunity for somebody to undertake a national or short course, careful use of a series such as *In Charge* can provide the skills and knowledge necessary for an improvement of supervisory/managerial effectiveness.

Chapter 3

What is Management Competence?

The *Concise Oxford Dictionary* defines competent as:

(a) adequately qualified or capable;
(b) effective

How does one judge effectiveness or capability? The traditional approach to management/supervisory development was based upon standardized inputs; a set course of study, knowledge workshops etc., followed by some form of away from work examination. This form of development was able to test how much the participant had understood the concepts but was unable to test for them in actual work situations.

A competence approach uses evidence gained either from the work place or from work related simulations to measure the effectiveness not of the learning but of the actual participant. To accomplish this requires a set of national standards against which competence can be measured.

A good example of a competence approach is the driving test. The examiner judges each person against a set of national criteria. How a person learned to drive is unimportant, the test measures whether they are a competent driver on the day.

However, to drive competently requires more than just undertaking a short test, it also requires knowledge and understanding, hence the Highway Code test. People taking their test do not normally do so using the exact right turns, parking exercises, etc. that they practised on so they need the understanding necessary to transfer from the practice exercises to those on the test.

THE MANAGEMENT STANDARDS

Just as the driving test is measured against national standards, so the competence of a supervisor or manager can be similarly measured.

The Management Charter Initiative (MCI) is the lead body for developing management standards in the United Kingdom. At the time of writing (1993), standards have been developed at three levels:

Standards have been developed at 4 levels:

Level 6   Senior Managers
Level 5   N/SVQ5   Middle Managers
Level 4   N/SVQ4   Junior Managers
Level 3   N/SVQ3   Supervisors

The standards allow a person to judge their competence in an objective manner by seeing how the way they perform tasks match up to the national criteria.

Because the standards are based more on what a person does than on what they know, they are of equal use to those undertaking a course of study and those who only wish to know more about their own effectiveness.

The standards, as revised in 1997, are arranged in 7 key role areas:

Manage Activities   Manage Resources
Manage People   Manage Information
these areas are covered by the *In Charge* series but there are also standards that relate to:
Managing Energy, Managing Quality and Managing Projects for those in specialized managerial roles.

The supervisory standards include the management of finance within the operations role as it is appreciated that supervisors/first line managers (FLMs) may have little day-to-day contact with the finance functions, although finance is included within the *In Charge* series because it is believed that those entering supervision and management will need an appreciation of the role finance plays within their organization.

Each Key Role Area is divided into a number of units which are further divided into elements of competence, as can be seen in figure 3.1. The elements contain a series of performance criteria and range statements relating to that element. Performance criteria specify the outcomes a competent supervisor/FLM should achieve whilst the knowledge requirements detail the relevant knowledge and understanding required and evidence requirements direct the candidate to the types of suitable evidence. These criteria and statements will be readily available to those who need them for the production of evidence as part of a formal qualification. One example is reproduced below.

Unit A1   Maintain activities to meet requirements
**Element A1.3 Make recommendations for improvements
                to work activities**

The National Standard

This section provides criteria to assess whether you *make recommendations for improvements to work activities* to the National Standard of competence. It also lists the knowledge and understanding which are essential for effective performance.

PERFORMANCE CRITERIA

You must ensure that

(a) you provide opportunities for **relevant people** to suggest ways of improving activities

(b) your recommendations for improvements to activities are based on sufficient, valid and reliable information

(c) your recommendations for improvements are consistent with the objectives of your team and your organization

(d) your recommendations take into account the impact of introducing changes on other parts of your organization

(e) you make recommendations promptly to the **relevant people**

(f) you present your recommendations in a manner and form consistent with your organization's procedures.

KNOWLEDGE REQUIREMENTS

You need to know and understand

Analytical techniques

- how to assess current working practices and identify possible areas for improvement
- how to identify the implications of change for other parts of your organization

Communication

- how to communicate effectively with team members, colleagues, line managers and people outside your organization
- how to present and argue a case for change most effectively

Continuous improvement

- the importance of continuous improvement in the management of activities and your responsibilities in relation to this

Organizational context

- the procedure to follow in order to recommend improvements in working practices.

NVQ and SVQ Assessment

This section specifies the evidence you must show if you wish to have your performance assessed against the National Standard for National Vocational Qualifications or Scottish Vocational Qualifications. It also gives some examples of evidence.

EVIDENCE REQUIREMENTS

You must prove that you *make recommendations for improvements to work activities* to the National Standard of competence.

To do this, you must provide evidence to convince your assessor that you consistently meet **all** the performance criteria.

Your evidence must be the result of real work activities undertaken by yourself. Evidence from simulated activities is **not** acceptable for this element.

You must show evidence that you provide opportunities for suggestions and make recommendations to **two** of the following types of **relevant people**

- team members
- colleagues working at the same level
- higher-level managers or sponsors
- specialists.

You must, however, convince your assessor that you have the necessary knowledge, understanding and skills to be able to perform competently in respect of **all** types of **relevant people** listed above.

EXAMPLES OF EVIDENCE

Here are a few examples to give you some ideas about the sort of evidence you might be able to find in your daily work.

Work activities
- presenting recommendations to team members and higher-level managers.

Products or outcomes
- project proposals, plans and budgets to which you have contributed
- your evaluation reports and status report printouts
- minutes of relevant meetings
- your briefing notes and presentation materials.

You may also provide short reports of your own, or statements from others who have observed your performance.

Written or spoken reports describing
- how you developed recommendations and the extent to which it was an individual or team effort
- the rationale and justification for accepting your recommendations and their associated costs
- the extent to which your recommendations contributed to meeting your organization's objectives and any other potential benefits likely to result
- the impact of your recommendations on other parts of the organization.

Witness testimony
- statements from people who saw you presenting recommendations.

MANDATORY AND OPTIONAL UNITS

Those wishing to undertake a Level 3 N/SVQ in supervision must complete 5 mandatory and 2 optional Units.

The Mandatory Units and the *In Charge* books that cover them are:

A1	Maintain activities to meet requirements	Managing Activities
B1	Support the efficient use of resources	Managing Resources & Information & Managing Activities
C1	Manage yourself	Managing Yourself & Managing Activities
C4	Create effective working relationships	Managing People
D1	Manage information for action	Managing Resources & Information

Optional Units covered by *In Charge* viz:
C7   Contribute to the selection of personnel for activities
C9   Contribute to the development of teams and individuals
C15 Respond to poor performance in the team
will be found in *In Charge* – Managing People

C12 Lead the work of teams and individuals has its first 2 elements in *In Charge* – Managing Activities and its final element on feedback in *In Charge* – Managing People
C1.2 Manage your time to meet objectives is in Managing Yourself and Managing Activities

DEMONSTRATING COMPETENCE

How do you demonstrate competence? In the main you can only demonstrate that you are competent at a task by carrying out that task to a defined standard. The *In Charge* series is designed around the Supervisory Management Standards.

There are only two states attached to competence:

Competent – having provided sufficient evidence of competency
Not yet competent – having provided insufficient evidence of competence

Those in the latter category are working towards competence.

Jean, whom you met at the beginning of this book, could use the

Unit		Element	
	MANDATORY UNITS		
A1	Maintain activities to meet requirements	A1.1	Maintain work activities to meet requirements
		A1.2	Maintain healthy, safe and productive working conditions
		A1.3	Make recommendations for improvements to work activities
B1	Support the efficient use of resources	B1.1	Make recommendations for the use of resources
		B1.2	Contribute to the control of resources
C1	Manage Yourself	C1.1	Develop your own skills to improve your performance
		C1.2	Manage your time to meet your objectives
C4	Create effective working relationships	C4.1	Gain the trust and support of colleagues and team members
		C4.2	Gain the trust and support of your manager
		C4.3	Minimise conflict in your team
D1	Manage information for action	D1.1	Gather required information
		D1.2	Inform and advise others
		D1.3	Hold meetings
	OPTIONAL UNITS COVERED BY *IN CHARGE* BOOKS		
C7	Contribute to the selection of personnel for activities	C7.1	Contribute to identifying personnel requirements
		C7.2	Contribute to selecting required personnel
C9	Contribute to the development of teams and individuals	C9.1	Contribute to the identification of development needs
		C9.2	Contribute to planning the development of teams and individuals
		C9.3	Contribute to development activities
		C9.4	Contribute to the assessment of people against development objectives
C12	Lead the work of teams and individuals to achieve their objectives	C12.1	Plan the work of teams and individuals
		C12.2	Assess the work of teams and individuals
		C12.3	Provide feedback to teams and individuals
C15	Respond to poor performance in the team	C15.1	Help team members who are having problems affecting their performance
		C15.2	Contribute to implementing disciplinary and grievance procedures
	OTHER OPTIONAL UNITS		
E6	Provide advice and support for the development of energy efficient practices		
E8	Provide advice and support for improving energy efficiency		
F5	Provide advice and support for the development and implementation of quality systems		
F7	Carry out quality audits		

Management Standards to put 'meat on the bones' of her job description. Her job description would tell her what tasks she has to perform, the Management Standards would advise her as to how she could judge her competence at those tasks. The *In Charge* series provides the under-pinning knowledge and understanding she will need.

An important feature of the Management Standards is their applicability across jobs, the same standards apply in public, private and voluntary sector firms and organizations, the tasks and context of the tasks change but the managerial competences remain as a constant.

To demonstrate competence, Jean needs to examine the relevant sections of the standards and see if she could provide evidence, if required, to demonstrate her competence. If Jean decides to acquire a supervisory qualification by a competence route she will be asked to provide a portfolio containing such evidence from her workplace.

Competence-based programmes are assessed not by the use of the traditional written essay but by the production of a 'Portfolio of Evidence', containing such items as work documents, personal reports, witness reports written by superiors, colleagues, subordinates and even customers. Should you embark on a formal competence programme, you should receive full details of how to build up your portfolio.

Unit/Element	Do I do this in my job?			Have I ever done this in a job?			How competent do I feel?		
	O	S	N	O	S	N	V	P	N
C7 Contribute to the provision of personnel for activities									
C7.1 Contribute to identifying personnel requirements		✓			✓				✓

For task: O = often S = sometimes N = never
For competency: V = very P = partially N = not very

Figure 3.2 A competence audit

In considering her competence and the evidence she would use, Jean needs to think about how relevant the evidence is, how current, and how it corresponds to the standards.

Each volume of *In Charge* commences with a 'Competence Audit' to allow the reader to assess what it is they do and their competence at it based on the National Standards. The 'Competence Audit' asks you to look at each element of the Management Standards and to consider whether you do that task in your current job, or have done it in a previous job, and how competent you feel you really are. A partially completed example of the 'Managing People' audit is shown in figure 3.2.

PERSONAL COMPETENCES

The competence standards we have looked at relate to the functions the supervisor/FLM carries out. They can be considered as *functional competences*, i.e. as directly related to the job the supervisor/FLM does. There are also a set of competences that relate to the personal attributes needed to be a competent manager at any level, ranging from supervisor to senior manager. These are known as *personal competences*.

The *In Charge* series covers both functional and personal competences and each volume contains information on the personal competences that are linked to the relevant functional competences.

Following the MCI guidelines the personal competence dimensions are grouped or 'clustered' as follows:

1 Planning to Optimize the Achievement of Results:
   1.1 Showing concern for excellence
   1.2 Setting and prioritizing objectives
   1.3 Monitoring and responding to actual as against planned activities
2 Managing Others to Optimize Results:
   2.1 Showing sensitivity to the needs of others
   2.2 Relating to others
   2.3 Obtaining the commitment of others
   2.4 Presenting oneself positively to others
3 Managing Oneself to Optimize Results:
   3.1 Showing self-confidence and personal drive
   3.2 Managing personal emotions and stress
   3.3 Managing personal learning and development
4 Using Intellect to Optimize Results:
   4.1 Collecting and organizing information
   4.2 Identifying and applying concepts
   4.3 Taking decisions.

Personal competences are harder to assess but should not be ignored. Much of the initial work on management competence was carried out by John Burgoyne and his co-workers and they developed a set of 11 areas of competence that they considered to be very important for those in supervisory and/or management positions. These are:

1 *Command of the basic facts*. To ensure that supervisor/FLM is well informed about organizational developments, customer needs, relevant data etc.;

2 *Relevant professional knowledge*. The supervisor/FLM needs to be aware of professional developments within the field of supervision and management and the potential implications of social, economic, legislative and environmental changes on their organization and their role within that and other organizations;

3 *Continuing sensitivity to events*. The skills necessary to become attuned to organizational situations and the analysis of situations from a variety of standpoints, and the capacity for further responsibility and the sensitivity to changing situations and demands;

4 *Problem solving, analytical and decision making skills*. Understand the steps involved in effective decision making, collecting and using data and monitoring processes and evaluating outcomes;

5 *Social skills and abilities*. Improving communication in the work situation, and to provide both strategies for the resolution of conflict and insight into team functioning;

6 *Emotional resilience*. To gain in self-confidence and provide strategies for dealing with stress and time management;

7 *Proactivity*. To improve flexibility and responsiveness to changing situations and demands;

8 *Creativity*. To enhance the capability to seek effective solutions to supervisory and managerial problems;

9 *Mental agility*. To develop the ability to grasp things quickly, to switch from one problem to another;

10 *Balanced learning habits and styles*. To develop a range of learning strategies that the participant can use to assist in the work situation and to manage personal current and future developments;

11 *Self-knowledge*. To be aware of personal strengths, weak-

nesses, opportunities and threats so as to retain a high degree of self-control over personal actions.

THINK POINT

Consider the eleven 'Competences' quoted above. Think of questions that you can ask yourself to see if you have a development need in that area, then place your development needs in priority.

The *In Charge* authors have examined a third set of competences, *organizational competences*, in other words those competences that the organization as a whole needs to possess for success, ability to react to change, seeking new markets, and so forth.

The role of competence in linking the overall goals of an organization with the tasks performed within the organization is shown in figure 3.3.

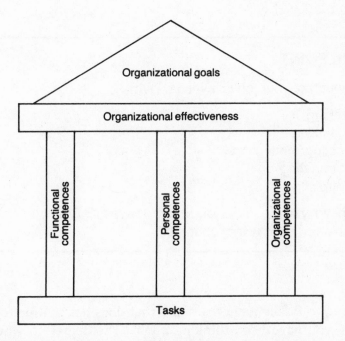

Figure 3.3 Organizational effectiveness – a competence model

One of the first questions often asked when somebody obtains their first supervisory/FLM job, a question that was uppermost in Jean's mind, is 'What will I actually be doing?'.

Supervision means taking charge: taking charge of people, operations and/or resources. Supervision and management can be described as 'getting things done through the activities of others'. Often it will mean having direct responsibility for others but in some cases one will merely be reliant on others, having no direct control over their activities but needing their cooperation in order to ensure that your tasks are carried out.

In 1916 Henri Fayol, who we shall meet again, defined management in the following terms:

> To manage is to forecast and plan, to organize, to command, to coordinate and to control.

A more recent definition, that of Koontz and O'Donnell in 1976, followed a similar line:

> The five essential managerial functions are: planning, organizing, staffing, directing and leading and controlling.

THINK POINT

How much of your job is involved with:

- Planning
- Organizing
- Directing/motivating
- Coordinating
- Controlling

Which do you do most of, which least of? Can you think of examples of each within your job?

It is rare to find a supervisory job that does not centre around the activities you have been thinking about. The degree to which they occur in the day-to-day situation will depend on the job and the organization, but they should be present in most supervisory situations.

To understand how these definitions work in practice, let us look at Jean's position in more detail. Jean and her organization will form the main part of the case notes in the *Managing People* volume of *In Charge*. The other volumes have different case notes based in different types of organization, but you should be able to transfer the ideas and concepts contained within the case notes into your own organization.

Jean is 38 years old and came back to work after raising a family 7 years ago. She works for a department of a large local authority and, prior to her recent meeting with Mr Rawlings, held a Scale 3 position in the reprographics section which serves the needs of the whole department. Trained as a typist, she has attended courses on word-processing and the technical aspects of reprographics, and as a Scale 3 had prime responsibility for the photocopying function. Whilst individual sections have their own photocopiers, bulk photocopying came under Jean's wing as did the arranging of supplies for all the department's copiers. Her new supervisory responsibilities as a Scale 5 involve her in taking responsibility for the work of the whole section which includes a central typing pool, document preparation and despatch, central desk-top publishing as well as copying under the overall direction of the Office Manager, Mr Rawlings, who also coordinates the department's secretarial and communication functions.

As a Scale 3, Jean was responsible for coordinating the work of a team of 2.5 staff including herself. As a Scale 5 supervisor she is responsible for 14 other staff.

The position is temporary because the local authority are in the middle of an organization review and some traditional posts may be amalgamated or even abolished.

Jean feels that she is competent as far as the photocopying side of her new position is concerned, but she is worried about her technical ability to manage the newer technological processes being introduced (especially the desk-top publishing). She also is concerned about how the staff will react to her promotion. Jim was a very popular supervisor and Jean often found that he did not take things as seriously as she would have liked. She is concerned that her colleagues might not accept her in a supervisory position; a worry which affects many newly appointed supervisors and first line managers.

Jean knows that the section works to tight budgets but she has had no financial training, so she is worrying about this aspect of the job which she believes will be completely new to her.

In situations like Jean's, a competence approach to development will allow a person to consider both what the job entails and what managerial/supervisory knowledge will be needed in addition to the relevant technical knowledge. She will be able to consider what she has to do (the *functional competences*) and what she must be (the *personal competences*).

SUMMARY

The chapter concentrated on an examination of the Management Charter Initiative 'Management Standards for Supervisors' and how they can be applied at work.

A competence approach to supervisory/management development assesses effectiveness from workplace-derived evidence; it is about what the supervisor can *do*, as opposed to merely know about; although to be competent, the supervisor/FLM needs the necessary underpinning knowledge to support what they do.

The *In Charge* series is designed to provide the foundations of the relevant underpinning knowledge for the Supervisory Management Standards.

The Management Standards provide a framework for examining competence by stating what it is that a supervisor should be able to do.

The areas of competence are structured into Units and Elements with associated Performance Criteria.

The difference between *functional*, *personal* and *organizational* competences was examined and Jean, who will feature in future case studies in the *Managing People* volume of *In Charge*, was introduced.

Chapter 4

Understanding Supervision and Management

There are 19 elements contained within the 7 Supervisory Units of Competence (see figure 3.1 again). Of the 19, no less than 10.5 are directly related to the management of people. This first volume of the *In Charge* series examines those 'managing people' competences from the viewpoint of the supervisor/first line manager (FLM).

Jean, who featured in the introductory section, will be used to provide examples of people management at work. The reader is advised to look back at the description of Jean's organization given near the end of chapter 3, so that the problems she encounters can be put into the context of her job and then transferred to the experience of the reader.

The chapters are not arranged on a one-to-one basis with the Management Standards listed in figure 3.1, as it is impossible to pigeon-hole the knowledge and understanding a supervisor/FLM needs in this way. Rather, at the beginning of each chapter is a list of the units and elements of the Supervisory Management Standards that the chapter is designed to support. Some elements will be common to a number of chapters, whilst some will be covered in their entirety within a single chapter.

THE MANAGING PEOPLE COMPETENCE AUDIT

This chapter of *Managing People* sets the scene by considering how ideas about supervision and management have changed over time, but first you should examine the Competence Audit in figure 4.1. There can be very few supervisors/FLMs who have not been involved in the majority of the tasks in figure 4.1, but how competent are you?

Unit/Element		Do I do this in my job?			Have I ever done this in a job?			How competent do I feel?		
		O	S	N	O	S	N	V	P	N
C4	Create effective working relationships									
C4.1	Gain the trust and support of colleagues and team members									
C4.2	Gain the trust and support of your manager									
C4.3	Minimise conflict in your team									
C7	Contribute to the selection of personnel for activities									
C7.1	Contribute to identifying personnel requirements									
C7.2	Contribute to selecting required personnel									
C9	Contribute to the development of teams and individuals									
C9.1	Contribute to the identification of development needs									
C9.2	Contribute to planning the development of teams and individuals									
C9.3	Contribute to development activities									
C9.4	Contribute to the assessment of people against development objectives									
C12	Lead the work of teams and individuals to achieve their objectives*									
C12.3	Provide feedback to teams and individuals on their work									
C15	Respond to poor performance in the team									
C15.1	Help team members who have problems affecting their performance									
C15.2	Contribute to implementing disciplinary and grievance procedures									

For task: O = often   S = sometimes   N = never
For competence: V = very   P = partially   N = not very
*12.1 and 12.2 will be found in *In Charge – Managing Activities*

Figure 4.1 The *Managing People* competence audit

THE ROLE OF THE SUPERVISOR/FLM

In the Introduction to *In Charge* we considered two definitions of management:

> To manage is to forecast and plan, to organize, to command, to coordinate and to control. (Fayol, 1916)

> The five essential managerial functions are: planning, organizing, staffing, directing and leading and controlling. (Koontz and O'Donnell, 1976)

Management and supervision as a field of study is a relatively new phenomenon. Supervisors and managers can be found throughout history, but it was only with the Industrial Revolution in the late seventeenth century and throughout the eighteenth century that supervision and management together with the study of how organizations work became a subject for serious consideration.

The increased mobility brought about by the development of the railways from the 1830s onwards brought about much larger groupings of workers in day-to-day occupations. Prior to this time it was rare to have employees numbered in the hundreds. Then suddenly large factories and mills were built, employing many hundreds of workers. The first major writers on supervision, management and organizational behaviour were born at about this time; Fayol (1841), Weber (1864), Taylor (1856). It was a time of rapid industrial growth and belief that new systems and ideas were required to manage the expanding organizations.

It was also a time of considerable scientific inquiry, and scientists such as Newton, Faraday and Darwin were seeking universal solutions to the issues that were being raised in their fields of study. Thus Newton was able to produce his laws of motion that went a long way toward explaining many of the observations of physics; the idea of the 'one overall answer' was in the air. It is of little surprise that the earliest writers on management and supervision also began to look for a set of principles that could have universal application.

WHAT ARE ORGANIZATIONS?

We shall be using the word 'organization' a great deal in this series and therefore we need to define exactly what we mean by the term.

Chris Argyris (1960) has defined organizations in the following terms:

> Organizations are intricate human strategies designed to achieve certain objectives.

If we think about the local authority Jean works for it is not difficult to discern its objectives. Outwardly they are to provide a defined set of services to those who live in its area. These services will have certain performance standards set for them and there will be financial limitations. The objectives come first, the organization is the human response to achieving them. Sections, departments, branches etc. are part of the system that has been designed to deliver the stated objectives.

A second definition in Pugh (1971) suggests that:

> Organizations are systems of inter-dependent human beings.

You may like to consider how the family fits into the above definitions. Most families are systems of interdependent human beings that serve to achieve certain objectives: for example, the continuance of the family name, education of the children, a better standard of living for all the family members, etc. The family fits the definition well as does Jean's local authority, it has objectives it must achieve and it is staffed by human beings who are dependent on one another.

There are a number of recognizable sectors in which organizations operate according to their objectives. These sectors can be recognized throughout the world:

1 Private sector organizations

These organizations have the maximization of profits as their prime objective. They can be divided into three types:

(a) Manufacturing: for example, ICI, Rover Cars, British Steel
(b) Supply: for example, British Coal

(c) Service: for example, shops, banks, private schools, professional sports teams, leisure centres

Many private sector organizations may fit into more than one of the above categories. For example, British Gas are concerned not only with the supply of gas from the North Sea but also with retailing both the gas and the hardware associated with its use. Thus British Gas is both a supply and a service organization.

2 Public sector organizations: for example, local authorities, government departments, the Health Service, colleges and universities
3 Voluntary sector organizations: for example, charities, Church organizations, amateur sports clubs

Prior to the 1970s, the different sectors employed differing styles of management but the recent trend has been a convergence to a more 'business' orientated management style, making the differentiation between sectors more difficult. Examples of this can be seen in the development of local management schemes in the education and health services and the management information systems employed in major charities.

THINK POINT

- Which sector does your organization belong to?
- Do you have to deal with other sectors in the course of your work?
- What differences do you notice between sectors?

At times we all have to work with organizations from sectors other than our own. Even if all our work is within one sector, as members of society we have to deal with private, public and voluntary sector organizations all the time: Our garage, our local council, our church, for example. Differences of approach, customer care etc. can often be very noticeable.

ORGANIZATION STRUCTURES

Charles Handy, in his book *The Gods of Management*, has looked at the various cultures found in organizations. Culture can be defined as the values, attitudes and beliefs found within an organization, what the organization stands for and how it is perceived. Public sector organizations had traditionally adopted a very different culture from, say, manufacturing or service organizations but, as Jean was discovering, terms like 'customer care' and 'value for money' have become as widely used in her local authority as they are in the local supermarket. There has been a gradual convergence of culture and style; much of it, in the public sector, a direct result of government policy designed to encourage a market approach and competition.

Jean has been involved in these changes. The organizational review that has led to her new position was a result of a decision by the local councillors and the senior management team to move to a more responsive, customer-oriented structure which will require Jean to consider the implications on her supervisory style.

The organizational structure charts that are produced may give a hint to the style of supervision and management that is being employed. A rigid hierarchical structure, as in figure 4.2, may indicate a bureaucratic approach, whereas a flatter, matrix approach (figure 4.3) may be indicative of a more flexible, project team structure.

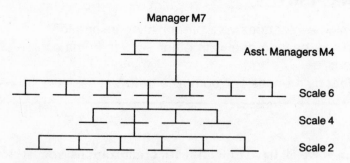

Figure 4.2 A traditional organization structure

Jean's department has decided to adopt the structure in figure 4.3, and with it many of the intervening grades will be abolished. This can cause difficulties with regard to promotion prospects, as the gap between grades may be perceived as too large for somebody to jump.

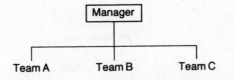

Figure 4.3 A 'flatter', team-oriented structure

THINK POINT

Which structure matches your organization? Try to obtain an organizational structure chart for where you work. Find out what major changes have occurred in the structure over time: what were the reasons?

Many structural changes have occurred as a result of new technology, legislation or changes in the type of business the organization is in. Structure should be adapted to meet the goals and needs of the organization and should not exist in a particular form because it 'has always been like that'.

One of the advantages of the more rigid hierarchy is that it reduces the 'span of control'. This concept relates to the number of people one person can supervise or manage directly at any one time. Research shows that it is between 3 and 20, though effective supervision occurs when the span of control is towards the lower level. To overcome this problem, organizations have tended to put in intermediate supervisory positions. Urwick (1947) believed that one person could supervise no more than 5 or 6 direct subordinates.

Jean's department used to have a structure like that illustrated in figure 4.4. The review has produced a structure like that in figure 4.5, with increased responsibilities for the supervisors and, hopefully greater flexibility for the newly-named support function.

The changes to the department are not dramatic but have served to bring similar functions closer together and have eliminated one tier of management, so that the supervisor of reprographic services now reports directly to the Manager of Support Services. The names of sections have changed to reflect a more customer-centred culture within the organization.

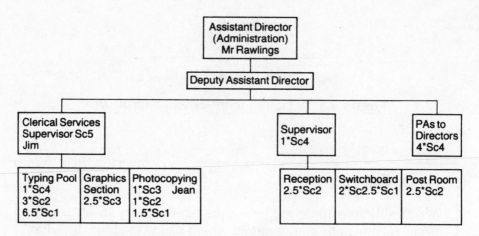

Figure 4.4 Jean's department before the review

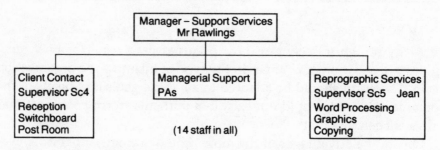

Figure 4.5 Jean's section of the department after the review

EARLY IDEAS ABOUT SUPERVISION AND MANAGEMENT

Max Weber, a German sociologist, developed an interest in how authority was exercised in the newly emerging large organizations. He concluded that as organizations grew, a formal hierarchy was necessary if they were to meet their objectives. Weber coined the word 'bureaucracy' for this type of organization. He did not say that it was ideal but that it was necessary at that moment in history.

Today bureaucracies may be thought of in terms of officialdom and red tape but in Weber's terms a bureaucracy was an organization that had:

- Clear rules
- A structure related to authority (a hierarchy)

- Specialized areas of work
- Appointments and promotions made on the grounds of competence and knowledge
- A separation between those who owned the organization and those who managed it. (In the private sector this is the distinction between the shareholders and board, and the management team; in the public sector this is mirrored by the differing roles carried out by elected members and officials)
- Fixed positions that would exist even if the postholder left or were promoted, i.e., jobs should exist in their own right and not be created for favoured individuals
- Rules, decisions and actions should be recorded in writing

Many a small family firm is run on very different lines from the above. Jobs are created for family members, promotion may not be solely on merit and rules, decisions and actions may be rarely recorded. There may be no distinction between owners and managers.

Weber's ideas were formulated with respect to large organizations and, whilst they have their uses, they have a danger of tending towards an inflexible organization. Rules take time to change and whilst a bureaucracy may be well-suited to times of stability, it may be a less comfortable place to work in the kind of rapid changes seen since the end of the Second World War. Large commercial and many, many public sector organizations developed into bureaucracies, and many of the organizational reviews undertaken in the last few years have been a response to the need for a more flexible structure.

There has been an appreciation that bureaucracies, concerned as they are with rules, position and authority, may not be very responsive to customer and client needs, and as we shall see, a customer-driven approach has characterized management thinking in the past few years. Indeed the use of words like 'client' and 'customer' would have been very rare in public sector organizations prior to the late 1970s. British Rail have replaced the term 'passenger' with 'customer' in appreciation of the changing nature of business. However, bureaucracy did form one of the first ways of managing large organizations and provided a structure for further organizational development.

Because bureaucracies have formal rules, hierarchies etc. they may be more resistant to change and thus better suited to times of stability. Both those employed by and the customers of bureaucracies have the knowledge that things will only change slowly.

The concept of customer care and internal/external customers will be covered in the *Managing Operations* volume of *In Charge*.

Henri Fayol, whose definition of management (To manage is to forecast and plan, to organize, to command, to coordinate and to control) we considered earlier in this chapter, produced his *Principles of Management* in 1916 after spending time as a mining engineer in the Belgian Congo. Fayol produced a list of fourteen Principles that he believed were capable of adaptation to any organization. You might consider them in respect of the organization you work for to see if they still have relevance. Many people believe that they have.

FAYOL'S PRINCIPLES OF MANAGEMENT

1 *Division of work*: given that universal secondary education was a relatively new idea in 1916, the lack of education of many workers persuaded Fayol that work should be divided up into simpler tasks that could be practised to encourage familiarity.
2 *Authority*: supervisors and managers should be given the right to issue orders provided that this right is exercised within the limits laid down by the organization.
3 *Discipline*: formal and informal agreements with regard to discipline should be part of the contract between employees and the organization.
4 *Unity of command*: Fayol saw organizations as pyramids with one person at the top from whom all authority passed downwards.
5 *Unity of direction*: given unity of command, the organization should ensure that all parts of it are moving in the same direction. We shall return to this concept when we discuss Peter's and Waterman's idea of 'shared values'.
6 *Subordination of individual interests to the general interest*: the general good of the organization should take precedent over the interests of any single group or individual.
7 *Remuneration*: employees should receive pay that is fair both to themselves and to the interests of the organization.
8 *Centralization*: Fayol saw benefit in bringing together the functions of the organization as this would make control easier. (The current approach is to decentralize and pass decision making down to the lowest possible level.)

9 *Scalar chain*: a clear hierarchy of authority running through-out the organization and ending at the top of the pyramid.

10 *Order*: Fayol, like Weber, saw the need for order and for ensuring that the organization put the right person into the right place based on merit.

11 *Equity*: Fayol realized that organizations need to consider their employees as more than just bodies who came to work and had no feelings or concerns. Equity represents the need for the organization to treat its employees in both a fair and kindly manner. This was manifested in the many activities and welfare facilities that organizations began to develop to assist their employees.

12 *Stability of tenure*: there is a need for employees to feel secure in their jobs and to be given time to master new tasks.

13 *Initiative*: within the limits set by a supervisor or manager's position within the organization, supervisors and managers should be encouraged to show policy initiative.

14 *Esprit de corps*: harmony, team work and a sense of belonging were considered to be vital qualities to encourage. Many Far Eastern companies have such qualities at the centre of their corporate culture.

Fayol's Principles are worth studying today as many supervisors and managers feel able to relate to them, they need to be adapted to the culture of the organization but they form a useful starting point for supervisory/management development.

THINK POINT

Consider Fayol's Principles in respect of your organization. Are they used, even if subconsciously? If so, which seem the most important today?

SCIENTIFIC MANAGEMENT

F. W. Taylor, who published his *Principles of Scientific Management* in 1911, spent much of his working life as a manager in the American steel industry. Taylor's observations led him to believe that because of fear of unemployment, fluctuation of earnings and the management's lack of principles, workers often restricted the rate of production to the lowest level they could get away with. He called this process 'soldiering'. It has an affinity with the work of McGregor, which we shall consider in chapter 5 of this volume, on motivation.

Taylor's employees were not well educated, and many spoke only rudimentary English because they were immigrants from all parts of Europe. He sought for a way to make the operation of the plants he managed more efficient and came up with the concept of 'scientific management'.

Taylor sought to measure each task, having divided them up into simple parts as suggested by Fayol. Workers would be provided with the most efficient tools available and then standard times and outputs would be set for each task. This would allow management to set a fair rate for the task based on scientific principles.

Taylor's ideas led to the concept of work study, which is easier to apply in manufacturing organizations than in service or public sector ones. It suits itself to simple manufacturing tasks but not to complex team efforts to provide services.

Scientific management would, Taylor believed, be beneficial to both the management and the workers, who would receive a calculable benefit from increased and more efficient production. It would be a fair system. Many managers on both sides of the Atlantic followed Taylor's principles and scientific management still lives on today in organizations which have a work study department using ideas from people like Henry Gantt (see *In Charge*, volume 2).

Scientific management might not seem to have much relevance to Jean's department, but it would be possible to set up standard times for day-to-day photocopying and it could certainly be used as part of the costing process. It is a relatively inflexible system, not well adapted to rapid change and a succession of 'one off' jobs.

THINK POINT

See if you can find examples of scientific management from either your own or organizations you know about. What kind of business are they in?

Scientific management techniques are still found in some manufacturing industries and especially where 'piece rate' payment systems (see *In Charge – Managing Finance and Information*) are in operation.

The ideas of Fayol, Taylor and their disciples form the 'classical school' of management.

THE 'HUMAN RELATIONS' APPROACH

Between 1927 and 1932, a team led by Professor Elton Mayo were carrying out research at the Hawthorne Plant of the General Electric Company in Chicago.

During a set of studies on the level of lighting on productivity, a General Electric team came up with a remarkable finding.

They were not surprised that when the lighting for a test group of workers was increased that productivity rose: this could be put down to working in a better environment. However, when, after a number of increases in light level had produced increasingly higher levels of output, they reduced the lighting to below its original level, productivity still increased. The advice of Mayo and his team was sought.

Mayo carried out further experiments by altering various working conditions (e.g. meal breaks) both positively and negatively, and discussing these changes with the subjects before implementation. The result: increases in productivity.

After a series of tests, Mayo concluded that the key factor was the involvement of the employees. There needed to be a modification of the classical ideas. Workers were not just units to be programmed to work; how they did depended on how they were treated as human beings. Mayo believed that the results of the earlier experiment could be explained by the fact that the subjects felt themselves special by virtue of being singled out as the test group. We shall return to this theme when looking at motivation later in this volume.

CONTINGENCY THEORY

There are obvious contradictions between the 'human relations' approach and classical management. Recent studies have concluded that there is no one theory of management; there are styles that are appropriate for particular situations and organizations. Lawrence and

Lorsch (1967) in the USA and Joan Woodward (1958) in Britain were early exponents of this 'contingency' approach – so named because the appropriate management style is contingent upon the situation and organizational structure and culture.

The supervisory styles adopted by Jean in a local authority might be totally inappropriate in a heavy engineering factory. Supervisors and managers therefore need to have a battery of appropriate styles that they can apply in the appropriate circumstances. This is why the knowledge and understanding component of the Management Standards is so important; transferability to differing situations and organizations is key to supervisory and managerial competence.

An interesting approach to contingency theory was that of Tom Peters and Bob Waterman, first published in their book *In Search of Excellence* in 1982. Looking at excellent companies in the USA they proposed a model for analysing the managerial situation. This has become known as the 'McKinsey 7S Framework' after the consultancy firm that was employing them at the time. The model is reproduced in figure 4.6.

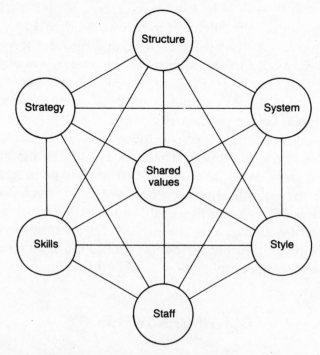

Figure 4.6 The McKinsey '7S' Framework©

From *In Search of Excellence* by Thomas J. Peters and Robert H. Waterman. Copyright 1982 by Peters and Waterman. Reprinted by permission of HarperCollins Publishers.

Peters and Waterman said that supervisors and managers needed to take account of organizational *structures*, organizational and personal *styles* of management, the *skills* of the employees, the actual *staff* available, the management *systems* operating in the organization and the *strategies* the organization uses to achieve its objectives. Change one of these and this will affect all the others. For example, the rapid introduction of information technology systems in the 1970s and 1980s meant that staff needed new skills and in many cases new staff were needed. This led to organizations being able to adopt new strategies and a reorganization of structures. New management styles were needed to obtain the most effective use of the above.

At the centre of the '7S' framework is the concept of *shared values*; those core values that make the organization what it is; they should remain constant and can perhaps be equated with Fayol's 'unity of direction'.

In looking at structure earlier in this introduction, it was stated that structure should change to meet organizational needs, a point well made by the '7S' approach.

THINK POINT

- Can you apply the '7S' approach to your organization?
- What happens if new skills are needed etc.?
- Can you think of changes in one area that have resulted in other changes elsewhere that this approach can explain?
- Have the values of the organization remained constant and what happens if they change?

One could argue that if the values change, the organization, even if it stays in the same business with the same name has changed beyond recognition. An example might be the newly privatized public utilities that have very different values as private sector organizations than they did in the public sector.

That concludes our brief history of the theories of management. The Management Charter Initiative is an extension of contingency theory. The standards give advice as to what the supervisor and first line manager should be able to do but the style adopted to achieve success will be contingent on the organizational situation. Using an appropriate style is one of the marks of competence.

SUMMARY

This chapter has considered how ideas about supervision and management have developed, looking first at classical theorists such as Fayol and Weber who adopted a systematic, scientific approach to management which concentrated on the division of work and the setting of standards for performance.

Whilst not directly associated with any of the Management Standards, a knowledge of how supervision/management has developed is useful in setting the work of the supervisor/FLM into context.

Max Weber coined the concept of bureaucracy. He considered it to be the most effective way to manage large organizations.

Mayo's work suggested that there were human factors at work in increasing productivity and this led to the concept of the human relations approach to motivation.

The most recent ideas have centred around contingency management, in which the supervisor/manager uses the style of management most appropriate to the situation and organization.

The following chapters examine a variety of supervisory/FLM functions, using the Management Standards as a vehicle for the consideration of ideas.

RECOMMENDED FURTHER READING

At the end of each of the remaining chapters in this volume will be a list of possible titles you might like to refer to.

It is not necessary to read all of the recommended further reading titles – use them if you wish to know more about the subject matter in the chapter.

Tom Peters and Robert Waterman, *In Search of Excellence* (1981).
David Buchanan and Andrzej Huczynski, *Understanding Organizations* (1985).

Chapter 5
The Human Resource

Supervisory Management Standards:

Unit C4 Create effective working relationships
         MANDATORY for VQ Level 3

Element C4.1 Gain the trust and support of colleagues and
              team members
        C4.2 Gain the trust and support of your manager
        C4.3 Minimise conflict in your team

This chapter of *Managing People* concerns itself with a broad view of why the human resource is so important and with the question often asked in supervisory/first line management (FLM) positions – 'what motivates people?'

Case Note 1

Jean was talking to her friend Ayesha.

'I'm worried about the amount of equipment I've got to look after: some of those machines are worth over £8,000 each; that's nearly half a million pounds worth of copiers, computers, printers etc.,' she remarked.

'Really,' replied Ayesha, who worked as a personnel supervisor for the same local authority, 'and what are your 14 staff worth?'

'They're priceless, of course, but the equipment was so expensive and it needs regular maintenance.'

'So do people, and let's do a few quick sums. I know the rough figures so here goes: The average salary for your section is £10,000;

that's adding up the whole wage bill and dividing by 15 including yourself. Some people have been there for 20 years, some are new; let's put the average length of service at 10 years. We could say that allowing for wage rises etc. the average salary over 10 years will be £15,000. Now add 20 per cent to cover employer's contributions to National Insurance, training, holiday cover etc.; that gives us an average of £18,000. Multiplied by 15 that makes £270,000. Add the costs of recruitment and induction and that means that the authority have committed over a third of a million pounds to your section alone in staffing.'

Jean was astonished: 'I hadn't thought of it like that.'

The hardware you use at work, be it heavy manufacturing machinery, a vehicle, computer systems or whatever, is a very important resource and needs to be looked after if it is to function effectively.

People are no different. They need to be acquired, installed, maintained and monitored. Like hardware, they need to be valued.

THINK POINT

- How long have you worked for your organization?
- Work out how much you have been paid in that time and add 20 per cent: how much have you cost the organization in wages alone in the time you have been with them?

People are an organization's most precious resource. Over the period of a career with the organization, employees accumulate a wealth of invaluable information about products, systems, customers, working practices, and so on. They also develop skills and expertise that are both expensive to replace and may be lost to a competitor if the person leaves. If an organization or an industry has to lose a large number of people in a short period of time due to economic factors, the loss of the skill base can make it very difficult to effect a recovery for that organization or industry when the economic situation improves.

THINK POINT

You worked out how much you had cost
tion earlier on; now add to that figure the cos
have been on. Remember you will need to add
course (you may have to make an informed guess) to
the wages you were paid for that time. You weren't at work,
you were being paid so at least part of your job would be covered
by somebody else. Can you also add on *your* estimate of the
worth of the knowledge you have acquired, knowledge that
would leave the organization if you left? This can include
contacts etc. that you have made for the organization.

Managing People is designed to give you the knowledge and understanding to be a competent person manager. It also looks at the
specific skills you will need to play an effective role in the recruitment,
selection and development process, and those crucial skills you will
need when conflict arises.

The ideas of Taylor and the 'classical management school' that you
read about in chapter 4 might be considered to have neglected this
area of supervision and management. Mayo's work with General
Electric highlighted the need for management to take account of the
human factor within the organization, and led to a number of studies
of 'what motivates people'.

It is worth taking a moment out from reading to consider the
following questions:

1 Why do I go to work?
2 Why do I do the job I am doing?
3 What job would I like to do?
4 What motivates me?

The usual, initial answer to question 1 is 'I need the money', but this is
a very simplistic response. Yes, we all need money, but what do we
need it for and is there a difference between what I need and what I
want?

The answers to questions 2 and 3 will be very personal but they will
be important in forming the answer to question four.

In the work situation it is important to consider the perceptions managers have about employees and vice versa.

Douglas McGregor, an American researcher working after the Second World War, considered that there were two possible perceptions supervisors and managers have about employees. Firstly, the traditional view was that:

(a) The average human being dislikes work and will seek to avoid working if at all possible;
(b) Because of this dislike of work, employees need to be controlled, directed and threatened if the organization wishes to fulfil its objectives;
(c) The average human being seeks direction and does not wish to assume responsibility; all that he or she really requires is a reasonable degree of security.

McGregor called this 'Theory X'.

His 'Theory Y' took the opposite viewpoint:

(a) Work is a natural human function together with play and rest;
(b) The average human being can learn not only to accept but to seek responsibility;
(c) Human beings link the objectives they are asked to achieve with the rewards they will receive, and such rewards are not always monetary;
(d) Most human beings react better to a reward system than a punishment-based one and can be self-motivating;
(e) The intellectual and creative potential of most employees is underutilized.

Common sense would suggest that if you treat your subordinates as though Theory X were the truth then they will eventually begin to respond in that way and you will only be able to achieve your objectives by coercion. Coercion only works in the short term. If you use it too often, people will either rebel or will leave at the first opportunity.

There are, of course, employees who seem to act as though Theory X was true; they seem totally disinterested in the job, do the bare minimum and need constant controlling, but they are in a minority. Consider the people you supervise: do they rise to responsibility, do they take pride in their work and their achievements? If so, it is much more likely that Theory Y is truer of the human condition. Perhaps it is something within society that transforms Theory Y to Theory X because most five-year-olds go willingly to school and are eager to learn and accept responsibility; it is only later that these traits begin to be replaced, in some, by those resembling Theory X.

McGregor considered that the average supervisor and manager was leaning more towards a Theory X perception of subordinates and that this was affecting organizational effectiveness through a wide range of undertakings.

Theory Y sees the employee as a valuable resource for the organization, a resource to be nurtured and developed. Theory X, on the other hand, sees the employee as a bit of a nuisance to be tolerated as the job cannot be done without him or her, but employees need to be watched very closely. Classical management equates in many ways to Theory X, later views of management are much more Theory Y orientated.

THINK POINT

- Which of the two McGregor ideas, Theory X or Theory Y, best fits your view of your subordinates?
- What effect could this be having on the way they work for you and on the way you carry out your supervisory duties?

MOTIVATIONAL FACTORS

Case Note 2

Jean had a problem. Organization reviews tend to lead to a great deal of documentation and one particular report needed priority treatment. She asked Mike, one of her staff, if he would be prepared to work overtime on Thursday night, when the last pieces of the report would be available, so as to ensure that it would be ready for the Council committee meeting on the Friday.

Jean knew that Mike wanted to buy a new video camera so she thought that the money would be useful.

However, when she approached him she was a little surprised by the answer.

'I have to go to my son's school that night, he's in a concert and it starts at 6.30,' he told her.

'But it is important that we have this report ready and I know you need the money,' replied Jean.

'No,' said Mike, 'it's true that I want the money, but I actually need to watch my son.'

There is a difference between what people need and what they want. Simply expressed, needs are internal to us, they are part of our functioning as human beings; wants are a more external influence, they are desirable but not necessary. For Mike, a new video camera would be very desirable but the need to undertake a parental activity was far more important.

Abraham Maslow addressed this issue and came up with the concept of a 'hierarchy of needs'. Maslow's work provides a useful starting point for a consideration of motivation. He argued that human beings are motivated by a desire to satisfy specific groups of needs that are arranged on a hierarchical structure (see figure 5.1).

The most basic needs are the physiological ones: a need for food, water, sleep, protection from the elements. These are the needs we satisfy first. If we are deprived of these needs our bodies may over-rule our minds. Sooner or later, no matter how important the job, if

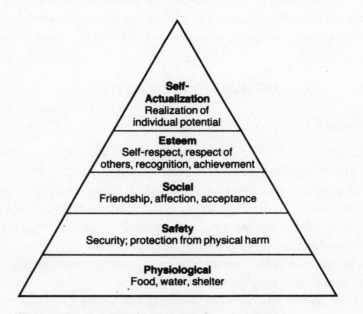

Figure 5.1 Maslow's hierarchy of needs

we haven't slept for a long time, we will fall asleep whether we want to or not even if we are driving up the M1! If you have a long job for somebody to do and it's nearly lunch time, let them eat first: a rumbling stomach is not a good motivator.

Having fulfilled the basic physiological needs, the next set of needs are those concerned with *safety*. This can encompass both protection from physical harm and such issues as job security. There have been countless cases of those who have been shipwrecked drinking sea water despite the fact that this will eventually kill them. This can be explained using Maslow's hierarchy by the fact that the need for liquid is a more basic need than that for safety. There is not much point in expecting somebody to be highly motivated if they are working in an unsafe environment; their physical safety will be of much more importance.

Physiological and safety needs can often be met in a physical sense but the rest of the needs in the hierarchy are much more psychological. After safety come the *social* needs, the need to belong and to be accepted. Inability to meet these needs can lead to withdrawal and anti-social behaviour. The short- and long-term psychological effects of 'sending somebody to Coventry' can be very damaging. Mankind is a social animal, as are other primates, and we need to know that we 'belong'. This manifests itself through the clubs we join, the emblems we display, our ideas about our country, etc. The family has an important role in fulfilling many of our social needs. Work on group dynamics has shown that a member of a group will risk the disrespect of others outside the group if that means remaining a group member.

Esteem is a higher-level need. Once accepted as a member of a group, the next need is to be recognized for one's achievements and the development of self-respect. Maslow's hierarchy suggests that those who are cold, hungry, feel unsafe and have been the victims of rejection will not be very concerned with self-respect and recognition of their achievements. Observation of events throughout the world would suggest that this is a fair assumption to make.

All of these needs – *psychological*, *safety*, *social*, and *esteem* – can be described as 'deficiency' needs. Human beings seek to remedy any deficiencies affecting these needs. If we are hungry, we seek food. The highest level need is a 'growth' need; it is known as *self-actualization* and is the need for realization of individual potential. Many people are not conscious that this need exists, and yet if met it can help unlock tremendous potential. You might think that it is a need only of the artist and the writer but it exists in all of us.

The Maslow hierarchy can be seen to operate on two basic principles:

- *The Deficit Principle*: a satisfied need does not motivate, we act so as to satisfy our needs;
- *The Progression Principle*: in general the needs exist in a strict hierarchy, a higher level need can only be satisfied when those lower down the hierarchy have been met. There are, as with all theories, exceptions. The artist who starves in a bedsit and concentrates on a work of art above all else defies the Progression Principle but the hierarchy holds good if considered in general terms.

Simple as it is, a knowledge of the Maslow hierarchy can be of considerable use to the supervisor/FLM because it can be used to explain the shifts in motivational factors that may be experienced with the same subordinate. In basic terms, an employee is likely to be motivated so as to to satisfy the lowest level unsatisfied need at that time. A change of job, domestic considerations, or worries about health can all cause movement up and down the hierarchy.

THINK POINT

- At what level do your current needs operate?
- Can you discern a change in level with your life circumstances?

Frederick Herzberg took Maslow's work further with his own model based on studies of American managers. His research concluded that there were factors at work that led to job satisfaction – *motivators* – and factors that prevented dissatisfaction – *hygiene factors*.

The major motivators were:

- Achievement
- Recognition for skills and achievement
- The work itself
- Responsibility
- Advancement and promotion

The major hygiene factors were:

- The organization's policies and administration
- Styles of supervision and management
- Relationships with superiors, colleagues and subordinates
- Money
- Status
- Security

Herzberg's findings are interesting in that they showed that factors such as pay and security did not lead to job satisfaction: a low level of pay will lead to job dissatisfaction, but once pay reaches an acceptable level other factors act to motivate staff, factors which seem to link more closely with Maslow's concept of self-actualization.

David McClelland's research found similar results, indicating that people tend to be motivated by their need for:

- Achievement
- Social acceptance
- Power

and that one of these tended to predominate at any one time. Indeed, power and social acceptance could be incompatible at times.

A supervisor/FLM such as Jean can use a knowledge of motivational theories to help them obtain the best from their staff.

Firstly, the supervisor/FLM needs to understand that what motivates one will not necessarily motivate another.

Let us consider 3 of Jean's staff:

- Paul, aged 22, has worked for 5 years and is in his third job. He is unmarried and still lives at home. He drives a second-hand Ford Escort and is an active sportsman. Scale 3 in the Graphics section.
- Helen, aged 48, married with two grown-up children. Helen is currently studying for an Open University degree in the Arts. Scale 3 in the typing/WP section.
- Alison, aged 18, first job. Scale 1 typist.

THINK POINT

What do you think their needs are and what will motivate them?

Paul and Alison will probably be motivated by money, but the fact that Helen is studying for a degree suggests that she is motivated by different factors. Perhaps her lower-level needs are being adequately met and she can now concentrate on the higher-level ones.

There are a series of steps supervisors/FLMs can take to aid the motivation process and to, in the words of the Management Standards, Unit 6: 'Create, maintain and enhance productive working relationships'.

1 Get to know your staff and find out what they want

Who are your staff, how long have they worked for the organization, what do they do outside work, what are their home circumstances? What ambitions do they have? What do they expect of you? How do they view their job and their position within the organization?

The answers to these questions will assist you in analysing the differing needs of your staff.

2 Show them how success can be achieved and help them to achieve it

Showing people a possible path towards what they want can help them to clarify their goals and how to achieve them. As a supervisor/ FLM it is vital that you link the achievement of individual goals to the completion of organizational ones. Praise staff whenever you can, praise works better than criticism. People learn more from successes than from failures.

Allow your staff some control over their working lives. This does not mean that you should surrender responsibility, but you can engender an atmosphere of trust and allow staff to have a fair degree of ownership of the tasks they are engaged upon. People who own something tend to look after it.

3 Build esteem and use suitable rewards

Many rewards, for example salary, may be fixed, but the praise that you give and the responsibilities you delegate can act as powerful rewards in themselves. Ensure that your staff feel that they 'matter' to you.

RELATIONSHIPS WITH ONE'S COLLEAGUES AND IMMEDIATE MANAGER

The areas we have considered so far have been concerned with motivating one's subordinates, i.e.:

Element 6.1: Create and enhance productive working relationships with colleagues and those for whom one has supervisory responsibility

Obviously, one's colleagues have their own needs as do one's bosses. Relationships between colleagues can often be difficult because of conflicting work and personal needs.

Case Note 3

Chris Preston, the manager of a professional section within Jean's organization, has come to see her regarding the production of a project report. Chris and his team have worked hard on a report that represents a radical new way forward. Originally due for presentation to the relevant committee in a month's time, recent pronouncements by the Government have led to suggestions that it should be presented during a ministerial visit next week.

Jean had allocated time for the report to meet the original deadline but the new deadline will mean that there will be a major disruption to other work.

Chris is clearly motivated to have the report out to present to the minister, Jean less so. The report does not affect her and she runs the danger of upsetting others in the organization by disrupting their work.

In situations like these, it is vital that the supervisor/FLM knows what is going on in the rest of the organization. Jean needs to take a 'helicopter view' that goes beyond her own section to encompass the needs of other sections. Chris also needs an understanding of the work of Jean's section so that he does not make unreasonable demands.

We can use the 'management continuum' that was presented as figure 2.1 near the beginning of this volume to show how the 'organizational focus' widens as one moves along the continuum (see figure 5.2).

The workforce tend to be focused on their tasks within their section or department, while supervisors and first line managers need to be concerned with the task, their own section/department and other departments within related areas of the organization. Middle managers should take a whole organization approach whilst much of the work of senior management concerns relationships beyond the organization's boundaries.

Supervisors should ensure that they know what is going on in other sections and departments and that they understand the needs of their colleagues within these other areas. Conversely, they should make sure that their departmental needs are known in other areas.

In addition to productive working relationships with one's subordinates and colleagues, the Management Standards consider the upward relationship vital to every supervisor/FLM:

Element 6.2 Enhance productive working relationships with one's immediate manager

The supervisor/FLM is a vital component in the communication channel between more senior managers and the workforce. In Jean's case, she must take the ideas and instructions from her manager, Mr Rawlings, and communicate them to her staff, whilst at the same time ensuring that the work of the department is prioritized and organized in such a way as to meet both Mr Rawlings' needs and her own. She also needs to pass on the ideas, feelings and perceptions from the workforce up to Mr Rawlings.

The role of the supervisor/FLM as a 'communicator' can be summarized as in figure 5.3. The influences on each level of the workforce, from most junior employee to the most senior management, are different. Whilst competent supervisors/FLMs will be very concerned with those influences that directly affect them, they will also be aware of the influences that are affecting their immediate managers and those they supervise.

It is important that one's immediate manager can rely on receiving prompt information about the tasks and feelings of the workforce, and that they in turn can rely on their supervisor/FLM to tell them of what is happening within both the department and the wider organization.

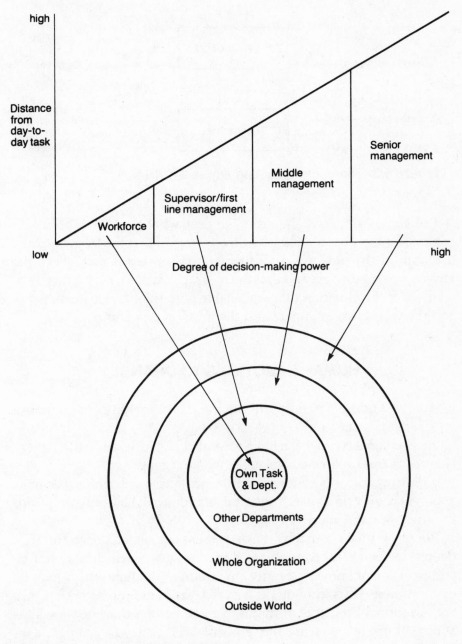

Figure 5.2 The organizational focus

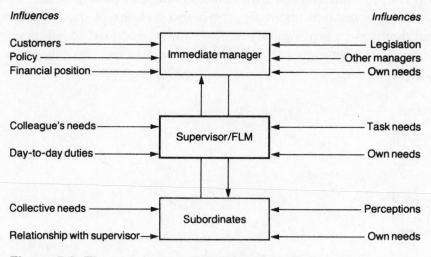

Figure 5.3 The communicating supervisor/FLM

The supervisor/FLM should not repeat what they have been told 'parrot fashion', but should take time to ensure that the language they use both in the upwards and downwards process is suitable to the message being carried, and that the message carries with it a degree of analysis of the situation that will enable both the immediate manager and the workforce to understand the implications of the message.

HUMAN REACTIONS TO CHANGE

Element 6.3 of the Management Standards is: 'Identify and minimise interpersonal conflict.'

Interpersonal conflict can have a number of causes and nearly every chapter of this volume covers areas where it may occur.

Within organizations, however, interpersonal conflict often becomes apparent during times of change, and as a subject it has implications for the study of motivation and trust.

However much we may wish for change, it is uncomfortable. People are being asked to move from a situation which may not be perfect but is a known quantity, to another situation which may be better though this cannot be assured. In times of recession and organizational problems, it might even be certain that the new situation will not be better for many people, there may be redundancies etc.

Because of their key position within the communication process, the supervisor/FLM has a vital role in ensuring that information about changes and the implications of them is passed to the workforce as accurately and as free from emotion as possible. They also have a responsibility for letting their manager know the feelings of the workforce. Again, language is important: management may say 're-structuring', the workforce may read this as 'job losses'. The supervisor/FLM should do all in their power to keep themselves appraised of the on-going situation as fully as possible, and should not be afraid to question their manager for extra information and to receive as much feedback as possible from their staff.

Misunderstandings and interpersonal conflict occur when people are starved of information; a good supervisor/FLM can act so as to ensure a smooth flow of accurate information, and thus short circuit the 'grapevine' of rumours that can lead to conflict.

SUMMARY

Supervisory Management Standards:

Unit C4   Create effective working relationships
MANDATORY for VQ Level 3

Element C4.1 Gain the trust and support of colleagues and team members
C4.2 Gain the trust and support of your manager
C4.3 Minimise conflict in your team

These standards cannot be achieved without a well-motivated staff. To achieve this the competent supervisor/FLM needs to understand and appreciate the factors that underpin ideas about motivation.

It is people that achieve tasks and objectives and thus competent Management of People is a key function of the supervisor/FLM. The creation and maintenance of effective working relationships and the minimization of interpersonal conflict are key tasks of the supervisor/FLM, the motivation of staff and self being key factors in organizational effectiveness.

McGregor's Theory X and Theory Y concept examined the perceptions that supervisors and managers hold about work and workers, and how these attitudes can affect the style of supervision and management.

Motivation studies commence from a consideration of individual needs and wants; the concepts of a hierarchy of needs (Maslow) and the Motivator–Hygiene Factor principle (Herzberg) form a useful framework for the supervisor/FLM to consider when addressing motivational issues.

The supervisor/FLM needs to be aware that different people will be motivated by different needs, and that the competent supervisor/FLM needs to understand the circumstances and feelings of subordinates if they are to receive effective motivation.

The use of the communications process in building up trust may be key to competent motivation. Such a process operates both upwards to the immediate manager and downwards to one's subordinates.

The concept of the organizational 'Focus' and the position of the supervisor/FLM shows how movement along the supervisory/ management continuum causes the individual to widen their view of the organization and increases the number of people they will need to build relationships with.

There are strong links between motivation, trust and the effects of change in reducing interpersonal conflict, links that the competent supervisor/FLM needs to understand and use.

RECOMMENDED FURTHER READING

E. C. Eyre, *Mastering Basic Management* (1991), chapter 13.
David Whetton and Kim Cameron, *Developing Management Skills* (1982), chapter 6.

Chapter 6

Recruitment and Selection

Supervisory Management Standards:

Unit C7 Contribute to the selection of personnel for activities
OPTIONAL for VQ Level 3

Element C7.1 Contribute to identifying personnel
requirements
C7.2 Contribute to selecting required personnel

Case Note 4

Jean and Mr Rawlings were in their weekly planning meeting.

'We've two vacancies in your section Jean,' remarked Mr Rawlings, 'I'd like you to talk with the Personnel Section about filling them as soon as possible. I'm sure that the temporary staff are doing a good job, but now we've had permission for the new structure to become permanent, I'd like to have permanent staff as well.'

'But mine's only a temporary post,' replied Jean.

'Yes, I know, and that's something else we need to look at. As part of our "Equal Opportunities Policy", your job is being advertised and I would like you to apply. You've been the supervisor for two months now, how are you enjoying it?'

'It's very interesting but these vacancies, I've never been involved in anything like that before – what do I do?'

'Don't worry,' he replied. 'You and I, with the Personnel Section, will work it out, and you need to think about your application for the permanent supervisor post – I'm more than happy to act as your referee.'

THINK POINT

How would you define a person's job?

A person's job can be considered as the set of tasks that the organization employs that person to carry out as part of the 'Contract of Employment', which we shall examine both later in this chapter and again when we consider the nature of the discipline and grievance process.

As tasks change over time, due to varying organizational needs, new products and services, new technology etc., so it must follow that a 'job' is not fixed permanently at the time of appointment but also will need to change as the tasks contained within it and the skills needed to carry them out change.

Recruitment, selection and development are key functions within any organization. The aim should be to ensure that the organization recruits and retains staff who possess the necessary skills, aptitudes and adaptability to enable the organization to meet its objectives.

This chapter is not designed to make you an expert on all aspects of the topic – that would require a very large volume to itself – but rather to illustrate the ways in which the supervisor/first line manager (FLM) can, as required by the Management Standards, contribute to the processes involved. It centres upon the recruitment of individuals. (The implications of recruitment for teams are covered in chapter 8.)

The process is more than just the advertising for and interviewing of prospective employees. A vacancy provides an opportunity to evaluate the position within the organization and to make decisions that will affect the future.

Case Note 5

Mr Rawlings and Jean were with Ayesha Mughal from the Personnel Department. Jean was quite surprised by the questions Ayesha was asking. She'd expected the meeting to be about the advertisement and the timetable for applications and interviews, instead Ayesha wanted to know:

- Why the jobs were needed?
- What kind of person was required?
- What skills were likely to be needed over the next five years?

'We want two word processing typists,' said Jean. 'They're to replace two people who are leaving, they're not new positions.'

'Have you really thought about what you need?' replied Ayesha. 'Do you want straight replacements or are there any forthcoming developments that changing these posts could help facilitate?'

Jean and Mr Rawlings decided to think about their needs for a couple of days in order that they could be exactly sure about the needs of the section.

Ayesha was quite right to draw Jean's attention to the possibilities for the organization that exist when appointments are being made. The process of acquiring staff is a complex one and can be costly, especially if the wrong person is employed.

The recruitment and selection process can be illustrated by the model in figure 6.1. The Management Standards refer to the supervisor/FLM as: 'Contributing to the identification of personnel requirements', 'Contributing to the selection of personnel' and, in Unit 4, with regard to 'Development Activities'. It is those three areas that this chapter will concentrate upon.

The recruitment, selection and development process will be examined through the contribution of Jean, who is not only being

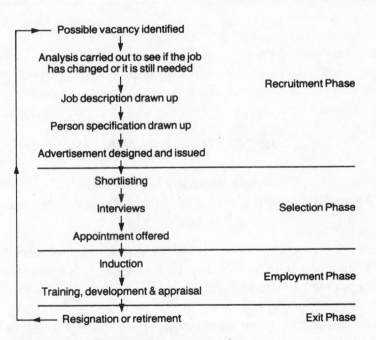

Figure 6.1 The employment cycle

asked to 'contribute' to the process but is also involved in making a job application herself.

How much you, as an individual supervisor/FLM will be able to 'contribute' to the process will depend on the policies of your organization. Many supervisors have little say in the appointments that are made; the *In Charge* team would argue that this is not a sensible organizational policy, as the supervisor should be involved with the appointment of staff that he or she will be supervising. Even if you are not closely involved with the process at the present time, a knowledge of how it works will be beneficial as your career progresses and you find yourself in the position of having a greater and greater say in appointments.

THINK POINT

- How much do you know about recruitment and selection policies in your organization?
- Who is involved and what contribution do you make?
- Do you contribute to the appointment of staff you will be supervising?

Using the problems confronting Jean, this section of *In Charge* will examine each aspect of the employment cycle in respect of the contribution that the individual supervisor/FLM can make.

RECRUITMENT PHASE

Possible vacancy identified; Analysis carried out to see if the job has changed or if it is still needed

Jean was concerned about the mechanics of *replacing* two members of staff. When a possible vacancy occurs, it is a good idea to look at the post that is being vacated to see:

- Are the functions that were being carried out still going to be needed?

- Is the position changing such that new skills will be needed in the near future?
- Can the job be combined with another job that may also be undergoing a change?

It is unlikely that a supervisor/FLM will be asked to carry out a full analysis of the functions within a particular job, a process known as 'job analysis', but you will probably find it useful to make a list of the tasks that your staff carry out, how frequently they are carried out and how long they take. Such a list should be updated at regular intervals to ensure that it reflects the job as it is and not how it was some time ago.

THINK POINT

Consider your job: list the main tasks you carry out together with their frequency and the average daily, weekly or monthly time you spend on them.

How have the functions and responsibilities of your job changed:

- Since you first started?
- In the past year?

Case Note 6

Jean's department has seen tremendous changes over the past few years, with new technology making some tasks redundant and creating the opportunity for others – word processing, desk-top publishing, high technology colour photocopying being just three examples.

Jean needs to ensure that the staff she helps recruit have skills for both today and tomorrow, not today and yesterday.

When Jean carried out her mini 'job analysis', following advice from Ayesha, she found that the amount of word processing the section was handling was actually decreasing due to the fact that many managers were using their personal computers as word processors, but that desk-top publishing and more advanced graphics work was on the increase.

She discussed this with Ayesha and they decided that rather than advertise for two standard word processing operatives, they would make one permanent appointment for such a post and a temporary, one-year appointment for a desk-top publishing/graphics post. The latter would be temporary as they were concerned that the individual sections would be able to decide to carry out much of this work 'in-house' in addition to the word processing they were already under-taking.

Jean presented this proposal to Mr Rawlings, who agreed and asked her to draw up a 'job description' and a 'person specification' for each of the two posts.

At the same time he gave Jean a copy of the job description and person specification for her own post: the one she would have to apply for under the 'Equal Opportunities Policy' operated by her employers.

Job description drawn up

A job description is a document that lists the areas of responsibility attached to a job and the functions that the job holder is expected to carry out. It is not concerned with the qualities of the person appointed to the job: these are considered in the person specification, which will be discussed later.

Although it is unlikely that a supervisor/FLM will be required to draw up a job description from scratch, it is possible that he or she will be consulted about the items to be included

It is important that the job description is not made too specific. As the last section suggested, jobs change over time and job descriptions need to be of sufficient flexibility to reflect this as well as being useful in telling the job holder what to do.

Case Note 7

Mr Rawlings had asked Jean to liaise with Ayesha to draw up a set of items to be included in the job description.

Jean had wished to make it very clear to the job holder the exact nature of the duties expected of them.

'. . . then if there are any problems, we'll have an exact record of what they are supposed to do, they won't be able to say that such and such isn't part of their job. For example, the word processing full-time post requires the person to produce letters, documents, reports etc. using "Word Perfect" (a word processing software package in common use) on IBM (International Business Machines) compatible machinery.'

'True,' replied Ayesha, 'but they could claim that that was all they had to do. Perhaps the item should require them to draw up letters, documents and reports in the organizational house style using word processing facilities. Then if we change either the systems or the software, people will not feel that using the new ones goes beyond their job description.'

A useful job description (often written as 'JD') should contain the following information (alongside it as an example is the job description for Jean's post):

Job title	Supervisor; Clerical Support
Job grade	Scale 5
Location	County Hall
Date of this JD	12.11.1992
Immediate superior/ line manager	Manager Support Services (Mr Rawlings)
Number of staff supervised	14
Overall purpose of job	To supervise the work of the reprographics, graphics, typing/word processing section of support services
Key tasks	Day-to-day supervision of staff; ensuring that hardware receives proper and prompt maintenance. Supervision of the: word processing, desktop publishing, graphics and reprographics functions of the section. Keeping records of work done; ensuring that delivery times are met; maintaining work flow records; ensuring that there are adequate supplies of stock and the ordering of new stock; maintaining expenditure records. Any other duties that the line manager may reasonably require.
Authority	Ordering of stock and routine maintenance up to £500

Using the above framework allows the job applicant to see exactly what is involved in the job, who they report to, how many staff they are supervising, what the key tasks are and how much authority they have. Note the 'Any other duties that the line manager may reasonably require' clause under 'Key tasks'. The definition of reasonable may often be a source of conflict, and may need to be the subject of negotiation between the employee and the supervisor/FLM and their superior.

THINK POINT

- Do you have a formal job description?
- Does it fit the pattern considered above?
- If not, as an exercise rewrite it using Jean's JD as a model – does it provide a clearer picture of your job in this format?

Person specification drawn up

The JD provides a list of key tasks and gives a context to the job. The Person Specification is a document that outlines the skills and personal qualities needed to carry out the job.

A well-written person specification divides the skills and personal qualities into two areas: those that are essential and those that are desirable in an applicant.

As in the last section, suitable headings, together with a sample person specification for Jean's job, using the Rodger (1952) '7 Point Plan' are illustrated below.

Job title   Supervisor; Clerical Support
Job grade   Scale 5
Location   County Hall
Date of this person
  specification   12.11.1992
Immediate superior/   Manager Support Services (Mr Rawlings)
  line manager
Number of staff
  supervised   14
Overall purpose of job   To supervise the work of the reprographics, graphics, typing/word processing section of support services

	Essential	Desirable
Physical appearance	Neat, clean appearance	None in particular
Qualifications	GCE 'O' Level or GCSE in English and Maths Clean driving licence	Typing/word processing

Aptitudes	Ability to relate to staff	Computerate
Intelligence	Quick thinking	None in particular
Disposition	Calm and collected in a crisis, able to absorb new information	Sense of humour
Interests	None in particular	Interest in computing
Circumstances	Must be able to work on a flexi-time basis, with some evening duties	None in particular

The person specification need not be detailed but it does give intending applicants a broader view of what the job involves and whether their skills, aptitudes etc. fit them for it.

In a way it acts as a first filter in the selection process, if a copy is sent out with the job description and application form, as those who do not meet the person specification are less likely to apply for the job than those who do. Where the person specification is not made public, then the advertisement will often give intending applicants clues as to the type of person required. Note that in Jean's case, the person specification does not specify which word processing qualifications are considered desirable, because computer software changes: a positive aptitude towards change and a knowledge of new technology will allow for suitable training and development to take place. Note also that as this is a person specification for a supervisor position, skills relating to people management are deemed to be more important than task related ones.

The balance between essential and desirable items is important, because if it is weighted towards the 'essential', many possible applicants may be put off applying by the restrictive nature of the person specification. Clearly there will be times when the qualifications needed for a post are very exacting and it would be a waste of time for anybody without them to apply.

THINK POINT

Draw up a person specification for a job in your section or department – what items do you consider 'essential' and which 'desirable'? Are you being realistic in framing your essential items?

Advertisement designed and issued

It is highly unlikely that the supervisor/FLM will draw up and place an advertisement. This is normally a function of the Personnel Department or Section, but he or she may be asked for advice on where to place the advertisement.

If the person specification has been drawn up correctly, there will be no problem in framing the advertisement to attract suitably qualified candidates, but there may need to be specialist input as to the correct placement.

Placing an advertisement can be an additional filter in the selection process. People can only apply for jobs they know about!; thus there are a number of possible alternatives, depending on the local job situation and the likely availability of suitable applicants:

1. **Internal**   Here the job is only advertised within the organization. 'Internal only' appointments are often made when an organization is over-staffed and should not be recruiting from outside at the same time as shedding staff.

The danger with making an appointment using internal recruitment only is that one may have to compromise on skills etc., if some areas of the person specification are missing from the applications. There is also a loss of outside expertise coming into the organization.

The restriction of advertisements to an internal only audience can be against the 'Equal Opportunities' policies practised by many organizations, and it is often a compromise to advertise both internally and locally. All advertisements should be communicated to your own staff via newsletters, vacancy sheets and notice boards, in addition to any outside advertising.

2. **Local**   If the skills required are likely to be found in the local area, then it may only be necessary to advertise in the local newspapers. This has the advantages of lowering the costs of the advertisement, the expense costs for interviews and any relocation costs to be paid to the successful applicant. One can always widen the net if sufficient suitable applications are not received.

The local Job Centre should also be informed of any vacancies so that they can advertise them.

3. **National**   Many large organizations advertise in the national press so as to attract a wider range of candidates. It can be a costly

process, as the advertisements are more expensive, interview expenses will be greater and large relocation costs may be incurred. The higher the post level, the more likely is national and even international advertising.

4. International With the advent of the Single European Market, many more international advertisements are being placed so as to widen the candidate net even further. These are unlikely to affect many supervisors/FLMs, although those in the defence, transportation, construction, health and energy industries may well find that their skills are being recruited from further afield.

5. Specialist Trade and professional magazines may provide an ideal forum for targeting a job advertisement, as only those already concerned with the field of work in question are likely to read them. This can be a very cost effective form of advertising for job vacancies.

Vacancies cost money. There are the costs involved in analysis, drawing up job descriptions and person specifications, advertising, interviews, relocation, induction and training. The aim of advertising, therefore, should be to ensure that sufficient suitable candidates apply whilst at the same time minimizing costs. The supervisor/FLM can use his or her knowledge of the job to assist in making the targeting of advertisements as precise as possible.

THINK POINT

- Where would you advertise your job in order to attract suitable candidates? Bear in mind cost and look for the most cost effective means.
- How would you word the advertisement?

Case Note 8

In January 1993 the following advertisement appeared in the vacancy newsletter of Jean's organization and five local newspapers:

—————— Metropolitan Council
Support Services Department
Town Hall ——————
Post of Supervisor – Clerical Support Section

Scale 5 £9000 – £12,000 pa

Applications are invited for the above post which has arisen due to the re-organization of the Council's functions.

The successful applicant will be responsible for 14 staff and the day-to-day supervision of clerical, word processing, reprographics, desk-top publishing and graphics work in a section which serves a number of Service Delivery Departments.

Applicants should possess GCE 'O' Level/GCSE (or equivalent) in English and Mathematics together with a sound knowledge of modern office working practices.

The successful applicant should possess proven supervisory skills and have the ability to relate to staff and to be an effective leader of a team.

Some evening work is required and, as there will be a need to visit outlying offices, a clean driving licence is essential.

An application pack including an application form, job description and person specification is available from and should be returned to:
The Personnel Department
quoting reference CSS/S/459
The closing date for applications is: 12 February 1993
—————— Metropolitan Council is an 'Equal Opportunities' employer

This ends our consideration of the first phase of the employment cycle, the recruitment phase. Hopefully applications from suitable persons are coming in. How these are handled and an appointment made, and the contribution that the supervisor/FLM can make are considered next.

SELECTION PHASE

Shortlisting

The days when involvement in the selection process was deemed to be a middle/senior management task only appear to be receding quickly.

Many, if not the majority, of organizations now involve their supervisors/FLMs in the recruitment and selection process. Shortlisting of applicants is a crucial element in the selection phase.

Case Note 9

Thursday morning and Ayesha brought over a stack of more than thirty completed application forms and accompanying letters.

'That reminds me,' remarked Jean, 'I must put my application in. I'll finish it off tonight; I've received the form and filled it in, I've only the letter of application to write now.'

'Well you'd better start looking at these. I've photocopied a set for you and a set for Mr Rawlings. Can you two get together and let me have the shortlist on Wednesday?' Ayesha said, as she hurried out of the door.

That evening Jean had two tasks, firstly she had to write a letter to accompany her application and secondly she would need to consider the forms and letters she had received from Ayesha.

Before starting on her letter, curiosity got the better of Jean and she started to glance at the letters for the two posts in her section.

Some were well-presented and laser printed, some had beautiful handwriting, one or two she couldn't read and one was actually written on lined exercise paper!

'Well, that one's out for a start,' she thought.

THINK POINT

How would you feel if you received a letter of application that was badly written or written on exercise paper?

Most job applications require the applicant to complete a form, and many also ask for further details, either on the last sheet of the form and continued on added sheets or as a separate letter of application. This document should not be a repeat of the details on the form itself but should seek to fill in any gaps and to expand on any areas that the applicant feels need further explanation. For instance, Jean could expand on the way she approached her new duties on taking up the temporary position. Outside interests can also be included: most employers respond positively to applicants who have such outside interests provided they do not impinge into the workplace to any great degree.

Jean could also include a copy of her *curriculum vitae* (known as a CV) which is a brief (2 pages), typed career and qualifications history giving a short description of the tasks carried out in each position held. A CV is certainly useful for those applying for any form of supervisory or management position. There are a number of books, available from most bookshops, that give detailed advice on job applications and CVs.

For a job as a word processing operative, one might well expect the letter of application to be at least typed, if not word processed. Those shortlisting applicants should be careful that they do not reject people solely on presentation. It depends on the job that is being applied for. If the job requires clerical skills etc., then one should expect an application reflecting and supporting those skills; for other jobs the standard of application may be less important. For any managerial position, the standard of presentation, correct grammar, and so forth is very important indeed.

Once the applications have been received, they should be read carefully, by more than one person if at all possible, and considered against the job description and person specification. In that way, some applicants will be seen to have too little experience or the wrong skills and can be eliminated. Remember, however, that evidence of an ability and aptitude to learn new skills should be borne in mind, as you are employing somebody for what they can do in the future and not what they have done in the past; it is the gap in a candidate between current skills and knowledge, and necessary future skills and knowledge, that is important. How much it will cost to train this person and how long it will take them to get 'up to speed' are important considerations.

It is not wise to set a precise number of applicants to be interviewed before shortlisting as that can lead to either rejecting somebody you would have liked to have interviewed or including somebody to make up the numbers.

Case Note 10

'There are five people I think should be interviewed for the first post and only three for the second,' Jean told Mr Rawlings on Tuesday morning.

When they looked at their list, there was one person who was on Jean's list but not on that drawn up by Mr Rawlings for the first job, while he had two extras for the second job and hadn't included one of Jean's choices – a young lady named Fiona.

They discussed the lists and agreed to amalgamate their findings with the exception of Fiona, as Mr Rawlings was able to persuade Jean that Fiona's experience and attitude, judging from the application, was not at the level required.

'Right, Jean, ask Ayesha to notify the candidates of the interview dates and next week you and I will sit down and plan how we are going to handle the interviews.'

Note that during the recruitment stage those interested in the job were called applicants, after shortlisting they have become candidates, one of whom for each job on offer will become an employee.

Interviews

Case Note 11

'Jean, your interview will be on Tuesday morning, you'll receive written details later today, but we think that it's only fair that the candidates for the two junior posts should be told who their line manager is,' Mr Rawlings told Jean during their morning meeting.

It was a good thing that he couldn't read her mind:

'If they don't offer me the job, at least I won't have to go through interviewing these candidates – I'm dreading that.'

Jean's thoughts appear to be shared by many. Interviewing candidates for jobs appears to be more daunting than being interviewed oneself.

THINK POINT

Think about interview situations where you have been the interviewee – regardless of whether you were offered the job.

- Were some better organized than others?
- Did the interviewer(s) seem to have prepared for the interviews?

The secret of a good interview, whether you are one of the interviewers or an interviewee, is careful planning. There are three basic formats to interviews:

1 A one-to-one interview, usually with the line manager, for the job in question: this type of interview can tend to be fairly informal, although there is the drawback that the interviewer may miss things and may be too subjective about a candidate.
2 A two-to-one interview involving the line manager and another fairly senior member of staff, often a member of the personnel department. These interviews allow the interviewee to relate to two people and the interviewers are able to discuss the candidates in a more objective manner. There is less likelihood of things being missed.
3 A panel interview involving a group of three or more. Some local authority interviews – for example those for head teachers – have involved up to sixteen panel members. Whilst nothing is likely to be missed during this type of interview, it can be very daunting for the candidate and there may be difficulty in obtaining agreement from the panel members. If panel interviews are to be used, small panels tend to be more effective than large ones. Jean was to be interviewed by a panel of three: Mr Rawlings, his boss and a member of the personnel department (not, she was relieved to find out, Ayesha; it would have been too nerve-wracking being interviewed by a friend, in addition to laying the process open to charges of being unfair).

Case Note 12

Jean was very impressed with the way her interview was conducted. The panel put her at ease and the questions seemed well prepared and matched to the job; there were no 'trick' questions and she was given ample opportunities to express her own ideas.

There were two other people being interviewed, and they treated Jean a little warily because she was the person currently in post. At the end, however, after Jean had been offered the position on a permanent basis, all agreed that the procedure had been fair. The two unsuccessful candidates were asked if they would like feedback from Mr Rawlings on the strengths of their applications and their interviews.

Preparation for the interview process is as important for the interviewer as for the interviewee. Interviews are not just a matter of asking questions and then making a decision. Research has shown that unless the interview is carefully structured and conducted, factors such as appearance and even perceived attractiveness can play a part in making minds up before a single question has been answered.

Pre-meetings between the interviewers can allow for a detailed examination of applications to look for any anomalies. Is there an unexplained gap between jobs and what could this mean? The applicant could have been out of work, raising a family etc.; they could also have been in prison – this would be an area that needed probing at interview.

As soon as candidates arrive at the venue, they should be put at ease. If they are to be interviewed one after another, they should be offered refreshments and shown where the toilet facilities are. A quiet area where they will not be disturbed should be set aside for them to wait in, preferably away from prying eyes: people are curious about who they might be working with and for.

The interview room should be set out as informally as possible with comfortable chairs, but not ones that allow anybody to relax too much!

Those conducting the interview should have met beforehand to discuss strategy and to agree a chairperson to be responsible for coordinating the interview.

Research shows that interviews where the questioning is based on a careful study of the job description, the person specification and the actual responses from the application itself are more successful than more haphazard procedures where interviewers have their favourite question and are determined to ask it regardless of its relevance.

THINK POINT

Think about the last time you were interviewed:

- How structured did you feel that the interview was?
- How structured would you have liked it to be?

Different organizations have different house styles for interviews and it is important that the individual supervisor/FLM works within them.

Case Note 13

Jean, Ayesha and Mr Rawlings were preparing for the interviews. They divided up the questioning so that Jean covered the more task centred areas, Mr Rawlings considered more personal and general work issues and Ayesha coordinated the proceedings.

They decided on the layout of the room, times for breaks etc. Each ensured that their staff knew that they were not to be disturbed during the interviews. It had been decided that they would not have all the candidates arrive together, but that each person could return to home or work after their interview and that Jean would contact the applicants later that day, to either offer the position or to let them know that they had been unsuccessful in as sensitive a manner as possible. She would also offer a feedback session to any candidate wishing for it.

Asking questions is an art in itself. For the interview process it is important to distinguish between 'Open' and 'Closed' questions.

Open questions allow the respondent to reply in depth within a fairly broad framework. An example of an open question is:

'Please tell me the range and types of duties you carry out in your present job.'

Open questions usually begin with: why, where, how, please tell me, please explain etc.

Closed questions place considerable constraints on the respondent:

'Do you operate a compressed air system as part of your job?'

Closed questions can often lead to 'yes/no' type answers which may not be appropriate when trying to see if somebody has the aptitude to fit into the organization.

Open questions should be used when you wish to know how somebody feels about things; closed questions when you want a short factual answer.

Multiple questions, that ask for a series of answers, should be avoided:

'Why do you wish to change jobs at this point in your career, and what is it about this job that attracts you?'

Such questions could lead to confusing answers.

If the questioning is related to the job description and the person specification, the answers should lead the interviewers in the direction of the most appropriate candidate. It is important that the issue of how the person will fit in with the current work group and the culture of the organization is also addressed. Recruitment into teams is discussed in the next chapter of this volume of *In Charge*, but those involved in appointments should realize that however well-qualified for the task a person is, they are not likely to be successful if they do not fit into the culture of the organization.

Final selection is never completely straightforward, compromises nearly always have to be made. If a candidate comes near to the ideal as determined by the job description and the person specification, and if all of the panel is agreed, then that person may be your man or woman. If there is major panel disagreement, or if, after interview, there are major doubts about all candidates, then a hard decision has to be made. Do you:

(a) Appoint the best, bearing in mind that you may have that person with you for a number of years, or,
(b) Readvertise the post, with all the cost implications that involves.

There are no easy answers but if you are really unsure and that is a majority view, it is probably best to readvertise.

Appointment offered

Case Note 14

'Those were not easy telephone calls,' Jean remarked; 'it's far easier telling somebody they've got the job than telling them that they haven't.'

Jean had spent an afternoon on the telephone to the candidates. She had arranged for the two successful ones to visit the office next week and had then to break the news to the others. She had remembered Ayesha's advice: 'Never tell somebody they were a good second'.

THINK POINT

How would you feel if you were told that you were second – would this news please you?

Case Note 15

When people had asked why they were not offered the job, Jean had tried to be as objective as possible and to make them feel that it was not because they had a personal deficiency, but that their skills and experience were bettered by the successful candidate.

In the case above, the results of the selection process were communicated to the candidates by telephone. There are two other methods of letting people know. It may be possible to let people know there and then, although this involves keeping all the candidates together until the end of the process; the second is by sending a letter. The supervisor/FLM needs to be guided by organizational practice.

The offer of an appointment can be a very exciting moment for a person. If you are involved, remember that this person will be working with you for some time and that the process of *induction*, which is the first subject of the next chapter, should start at the moment of job offer if not at the moment of job application.

SUMMARY

Supervisory Management Standards:

Unit C7 Contribute to the selection of personnel for activities
OPTIONAL for VQ Level 3

Element C7.1 Contribute to identifying personnel requirements
C7.2 Contribute to selecting required personnel

Ensuring that the organization has the necessary staff with the right skills is of key importance. As the person who is likely to be closest to members of staff, there is an important role for the supervisor/FLM, whose contribution to this is recognized by the Management Standards.

The mechanics of the process start with the need to re-evaluate jobs the moment a possible vacancy occurs.

There is a major role for the supervisor/FLM in drawing up job descriptions and person specifications, and their use in the short-listing/interview procedures.

Carefully targeted advertising can ensure that the right applicants are attracted. Supervisors will possess considerable knowledge of the job and can make a valuable contribution to this targeting process.

The concept of the employment cycle provides a structure for the supervisor to consider his or her role, a role that will differ from organization to organization.

RECOMMENDED FURTHER READING

G. A. Cole, *Personnel Management, Theory and Practice* (1988), chapters 8–14.

Chapter 7

Induction, Development and Appraisal

Supervisory Management Standards:

Unit C9   Contribute to the development of teams and
          individuals
          OPTIONAL for VQ Level 3

Unit C12 (part of)
          Lead the work of teams and individuals to achieve
          their objectives
          OPTIONAL for VQ Level 3

Element C9.1   Contribute to the identification of development
               needs
        C9.2   Contribute to planning the development of
               teams and individuals
        C9.3   Contribute to development activities
        C9.4   Contribute to the assessment of people against
               development objectives
        C12.3 Provide feedback to teams and individuals on
               their work

Carrying on our consideration of the employment cycle, we now move into the *employment phase*.

EMPLOYMENT PHASE

This chapter concentrates on individual development, although many of the ideas are just as applicable to groups of employees as to individuals. A fuller study of the implications of the Management Standards on groups and teams is contained in the next chapter.

Induction

You may be puzzling over the idea that some form of induction process could start before a person has been offered a job.

THINK POINT

Can you remember your very first impressions of the organization you are now working for – when and where were they gained?

The quality of documentation received after an inquiry about a vacancy, the manner with which the selection process was handled, the attitude of staff met during the selection process, all contribute to the new employee's perception of the organization. First impressions are usually very strong and lasting ones.

Case Note 16

'Jean,' Ayesha called, 'the new staff start on Monday don't they? Have you an induction programme planned?'

'I'm going to show them round the office and the canteen in the morning, but I'm busy myself, I'm sure they'll soon get to know where everything is – they're very bright.'

'Don't you think we should be doing more?' commented Ayesha. 'We've gone to a great deal of trouble to recruit the right people, it would be a good idea to ensure that they understand what goes on and who's who.'

'Well, what should we be doing . . .?'

Induction of new employees is a very important process that is often, unfortunately, relegated to a quick tour of the work area, canteen and toilet facilities.

Staff are a valuable resource, and it is worth spending some time to ensure that they are acquainted with the tasks they will be carrying out, the people they will interface with, the facilities they can use, the products or services of the organization and its culture.

Many people in large organizations can go for some time without seeing how their job fits into the whole, and this can lead to misunderstandings and can be very demotivating.

A good induction process seeks to make the new employee feel comfortable with their position within the organization and to give them the picture of where their job fits.

An organization that cares about its people will be concerned to present an image of good 'people management' from the onset, and this should be reflected in the standards of recruitment and selection.

The supervisor/first line manager (FLM) has a key role to perform in the induction process; indeed, its success will probably depend on them, as they will most likely be the person responsible for its implementation.

The first day in a new job is nearly always traumatic. The new employee is probably worried about their capabilities for the task, how they will relate to their new colleagues, getting lost in the building, which facilities they can use and perhaps issues connected with holidays, pay etc. Induction, when properly planned and executed, can ease these worries. A less worried employee is a more productive employee. Productivity during a job can be represented as in figure 7.1. We shall refer to figure 7.1 again later when we look at training and development.

There is a problem that unless induction is carried out in a systematic manner, the time spent with low or even minus productivity can be longer than it need be. Although Induction takes time, it does tend to shorten the actual period before positive productivity.

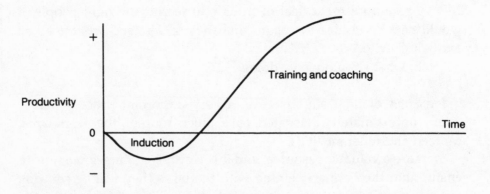

Figure 7.1 The productivity curve

During a period of minus productivity, the new employee may be making mistakes that actually cost money: in a production environment they may be turning out items that have to be thrown away because of defects, while in a service environment their mistakes may actually lose customers who may not return.

There is ample evidence that those who can see how they and their tasks fit into the whole operations of the organization are less likely to make costly errors, and this is of benefit to everybody.

Case Note 17

Jean was talking to her neighbour, Mike. Mike was a supervisor in a large chemical plant. The subject was the time it takes to induct staff, and if it was wasted time.

'We spend a lot of time on it,' said Mike; 'Every new member of staff spends half an afternoon during their first two weeks in another part of the plant. They're looked after by a member of staff from that department and that way they begin to understand how all the processes fit together. Everybody – operators, typists, drivers etc. – sees, and in many cases touches, the finished products. They also have a morning session, in groups, with the personnel manager and the general manager. It seems to work: our staff adapt to new tasks very quickly and we've a fairly low labour turnover rate.'

Many organizations have formal induction policies, but it is nearly always the responsibility of the supervisor/FLM to carry them out. Their attitude to induction can affect a whole department's: if the supervisor cannot see the benefits, then that feeling is likely to be transmitted to the new employee, who will gain the wrong impression about the organization at a time when they are most impressionable.

An effective induction scheme should aim:

to involve the new employee in maximum production within the shortest possible time, and to provide the new employee with all the information he or she needs to make an effective contribution to the organization.

A study of the above statement will show that it is actually about cost effectiveness, and that time and money spent on induction will be recouped by having a more productive employee in a shorter time.

An effective induction programme will have a number of ingredients and will not be a 'one-off' process but will feed into the training and development programme for staff. This latter will form the next section of the present chapter.

There are four strands to an induction programme: *task, facility, health and safety* and *organization*. These are illustrated in figure 7.2. Before we consider each of the four strands, it is helpful to think about who will carry out the actual induction process.

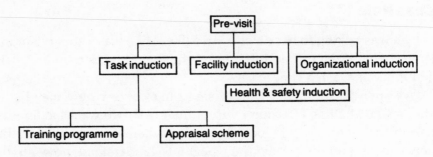

Figure 7.2 The induction process

THINK POINT

Who knows your job and what it entails best?

The answer is probably yourself.

It is useful, therefore, to ask somebody who has a job similar to that of the new employee to act as a guide (or *mentor*) for the first couple of weeks. This will be less threatening to a newcomer than their supervisor/FLM being with them for a great deal of the time. If you adopt this approach, however, you cannot delegate accountability for ensuring that the induction is carried out properly, you can only give somebody else the responsibility for actually doing it.

Pre-visit

Whenever possible it is useful for the new employee to visit the workplace prior to starting work for the first time. This is especially important if the time between appointment and starting work is of any length.

Such a visit should have the aim of introducing the new person to his or her colleagues and, if you have decided to delegate looking after that person to one of their colleagues, provides an ideal opportunity for these two people to strike up a rapport.

Do not try to provide a great deal of facts about the department/section or task at this stage – it is unlikely to be remembered. Make the visit more of a short social occasion.

Task induction

However well-qualified the new employee is, there will be ways in which the organization performs tasks differently to other organizations, and thus there will always be a need for some task training. Equipment may be different, different materials may be used and processes may follow different patterns. The first few days of the person's employment should include sessions with one of their colleagues (as mentioned above) working on the task to bring them up to speed and checking for gaps in their knowledge and training that may need to be filled.

The supervisor/FLM should arrange a series of meetings, perhaps after the first day, the first week and the second week, to talk over the employee's progress with the task and make training suggestions.

Facility induction

As a supervisor/FLM you probably know your office area and your building very well. Try to imagine how it might seem to a new member of staff who does not know their way around and may be very nervous.

If you have delegated the induction process to one of your staff or if you have decided to carry it out yourself, make sure that the people involved have enough time allocated.

Consider drawing up a checklist of items the new employee will need to know about.

THINK POINT

If you were starting a new job with a different organization, what would you want to know about the facilities?

Items that should be on your checklist, where appropriate, might include:

- Toilets
- Canteen facilities
- Smoking policy
- Coffee/tea facilities
- Break times
- Meal times
- Clocking on and off
- Lockers/coat facilities
- First aid
- Car parking
- Transport
- Machines/office facilities available
- Telephone calls policy
- Identity badges
- Uniform/dress policy
- Social club/events

These are all areas that people can become very concerned about. The use of a checklist means that you can be assured that the person has received information about them. It does not, of course, guarantee that they have understood – a problem we will consider in the chapter on 'managing differences'.

A useful approach might be to make up a little booklet on the facilities for new members of staff – check with your personnel department as to whether your organization already does this and how up to date it is.

Health and safety induction

Health and safety at work is covered in detail in the *Managing Operations* volume of *In Charge*, but it is important that the supervisor/FLM ensure that all new staff are acquainted in full with any safety procedures, safety drills, protective clothing etc. as soon as possible after joining the organization. Such an induction should be recorded on the employee's file.

Organizational induction

Departments of organizations do not exist in isolation. Organizations tend to be divided between what are known as *line* and *staff* functions. Line functions are responsible for the direct provision of goods and services either to another department or to the ultimate client/customer. Staff functions provide the support that the line requires in order to deliver the product or service. A production unit is clearly part of the line, whereas the personnel department is a staff function. If the two functions are to work together well, it is important that employees have a good idea of the role of the staff and line and how they complement each other. Marketing, a staff function, because it does not directly produce anything, may be criticized by employees in line areas because of the way of life sales and marketing staff often lead, but the whole organization should be aware that it is those sales that pay the wages; equally without line employees making a product there would be nothing to market.

It is useful if new employees can be given some time to visit all the functions of the organization possible so that they can see how their tasks fit in. If this is not a normal part of organizational policy, then the supervisor/FLM could make contact with his or her colleagues in other areas to arrange visits for new employees.

It is also important that new employees know about the wages, pensions and sickness benefits offered by the organization. The supervisor/FLM may have much of this information to hand, but if not then the assistance of the personnel department should be sought.

Induction may take up a little time but if carried out properly will result in an employee who feels that they belong to the organization and can see how their tasks fit into the total business of the organization. Ensuring that the induction is carried out properly is a key task of the supervisor/junior manager and leads naturally into their role in developing, training and appraising staff.

Training and development

Many organizations have their own training department, but this does not mean that there is not an important role for the supervisor/FLM. As the member of management most likely to be in day-to-day contact with members of staff, their training and development is a key responsibility of the supervisor.

There are three words often used when referring to this phase of the employment cycle:

- Training
- Development
- Education

These words all have slightly different meanings and implications for the employee and his or her supervisor.

Training is the narrowest of the terms and usually refers to a set of specific skills that the person needs for their job. Training can occur 'on the job', in company training premises, or through external agencies such as colleges of further education or training consultants, which may be used to impart specific skills.

Development Whereas training is related to the current job, development is more career related and concerns itself with achieving employee (or self) potential within a framework that goes beyond the current job.

Education is very personal and is concerned with ensuring that a person has the skills to make their way in life and society.

As in most cases, there are no clear divisions between the three, but one can perhaps say that the supervisor/FLM is likely to be involved in *delivering* training to his or her staff and *supporting* their development. Education is usually undertaken outside the workplace and is not normally work related, although some organizations (e.g. Rover Cars) provide financial assistance to staff who want to further their education even if this has no relevance to their work.

Case Note 18

It was the weekly meeting and Jean was reporting to Mr Rawlings on the training course she had attended on the new software package the section was due to start using.

'It was a very good course, but it was terribly expensive. I don't think that the budget can allow for all the staff to attend,' she reported.

'Why don't you send two of the senior staff and then the three of you can draw up a training programme for the rest of the staff. I'm sure that our Management Information and Computer Section will help,' suggested Mr Rawlings.

'Me!', Jean exclaimed; 'I couldn't train anybody.'

Training, like induction, costs time and money, and it is therefore important that it is carried out in the most cost effective manner possible. Unfortunately, especially in a recession, it is often training provision that is first in line when expenditure has to be cut. This may be a very short-sighted policy. Many employees see a link between training and recognition by the organization and you will remember from the study of Herzberg's work in chapter 5 that recognition is an important motivator. Organizations that resist cutting their training are likely to be better placed when the economy improves, as they will have better motivated staff equipped with the skills necessary for progress.

The benefits of a well-trained staff can be summarized as follows:

- Improvements to the existing skills base
- The provision of a pool of well-skilled employees
- Improved operations
- Improved service to internal and external customers
- Increased motivation
- Retention of skills and experience in the organization

These are benefits well worth having in any organization.

Training does not always involve long courses; it can also encompass short sessions on a piece of equipment, with the training delivered by the supervisor/FLM. It is important that those delivering the training understand the nature of the *training cycle* and have some knowledge about how people learn.

The training cycle has a structure very like that of the employment cycle (see figure 7.3). The relationship between the *training organization* (the provider) and the organization will vary. Some organizations will plan their own training and then ask others to carry it out; large organizations may carry out the vast majority of the cycle, including implementation, whilst smaller organizations may rely heavily on outside assistance at all stages of the training cycle.

Figure 7.3 The training cycle

Supervisors and first line managers have to work within the policies and structures of their organizations, but they can have considerable input into the identification, planning, implementation and evaluation of training.

The aim of training is to produce *learning*. Learning can be defined as a permanent change in behaviour.

Identification of training needs

Training needs may be raised by the supervisor/FLM as a result of their observations or from an Appraisal interview (see the next section); or they may be generated as a result of changes within the organization – a new product, new technology, legislative changes etc. Any change within a section, department or organization is likely to have training implications, and these should be considered whenever changes are contemplated. As was shown in the 7S diagram in the introduction to this volume, any change will have implications for the *skills* within an organization.

When deciding training needs, remember that training is not a reward: it should be there to aid both organizational and personal efficiency and effectiveness.

Case Note 19

One of Jean's new members of staff was well qualified on general word processing but obviously needed further training on the software used in the section. So did Alice, who was a very competent typist but was still having problems with the computer systems now in use. Both had the same training need but for different historical reasons.

The important task for the supervisor/junior manager is to identify the *training gap*; how it is caused is of less importance.

The training gap is the difference between the skills needed to carry out the required task and the skills the operative actually possesses. The gap can be filled using a variety of forms of training, as shown in figure 7.4.

Skills needed	Training gap	filled by	College course
			In-house course
			On the job training
	Skills already acquired		

Figure 7.4 The training gap

Any form of training should be planned. Firstly, training must fit in with organizational plans and policies; and secondly, it must meet the needs and aptitudes of those receiving the training.

The supervisor who is asked to contribute to the training and development of staff should consider very carefully what is needed, why it is needed and how it can be implemented to achieve maximum benefit coupled with minimum disruption.

Sources of training and associated materials should be investigated. Local colleges, libraries and of course the organization's own personnel or training department can provide valuable information.

Consideration needs to be given to the time of day devoted to training. Many organizations have decided to use a morning session because staff are fresher than at the end of the day. If the training involves a degree of personal development, staff may be prepared to give up some of their own time. Experience shows that this is more likely to be acceptable to relatively senior employees.

Work schedules may need to be revised, and the effect of taking time out for training on other sections and departments should be investigated, and any affected personnel informed.

A well-organized supervisor/junior manager will draw up a training schedule so that all staff can see what training is taking place, when it is taking place, the venue and who is receiving training.

Implementation of training

People learn differently and any training programme should reflect this fact. The supervisor/FLM is well-placed to assess the best method of providing training. Patience and the ability to speak clearly are prerequisites, but there are simple strategies that the supervisor can adopt to make training as effective as possible.

Firstly, whilst you might know the task very well, those you are training will not, and therefore it is important that new terms and procedures are explained carefully. Avoid using acronyms (words made up from the initials of a process or organization: e.g. NATO, VDU etc.)

THINK POINT

Think of some of the terms you use at work.
- How meaningful would they be to a new employee?
- How carefully are they explained to new members of staff?

Psychologists and educationalists have produced many theories of how people learn, many of these theories being the result of animal experiments extrapolated to humans. What is clear from the various theories is that 'practice makes perfect': the more often we do something, the better we are at it, up to a point. Familiarity and tiredness can lead to a falling off of performance. The model in figure 7.5 was encountered earlier in this chapter, when it was called 'the productivity curve'. Another name for it is 'the learning curve'.

When somebody first approaches a new task there may be more failures than successes, and productivity will be a minus figure.

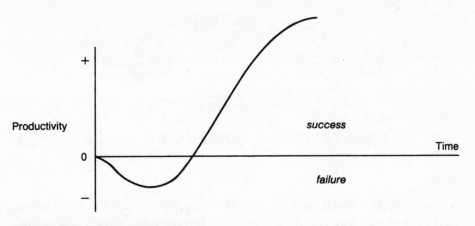

Figure 7.5 The learning curve

Research shows that a small number of failures, provided that there are some successes, can act as a motivator. As the person becomes more and more familiar with the task, the curve enters the positive and becomes quite steep: learning occurs rapidly. Eventually the curve flattens out at the point where it is impossible to do any better. There is a finite limit to most tasks – e.g., a human being can only type so fast however competent they are. The limits may be set by physical, human or mechanical constraints. The curve may dip slightly as the job becomes routine and familiarity, boredom and tiredness cause mistakes to creep in.

One of the key roles of anybody involved in training staff is to ensure that the time spent in the negative part of the learning curve is as short as possible and that the person being trained receives some success. Too much failure and not enough success can act as a powerful demotivator.

There are a number of advantages to learning at work: the surroundings are familiar; there is support from colleagues, supervisors and managers; the relevance of the learning to the job can be seen easily.

Where the supervisor/FLM has to be involved in the training, it is necessary to be aware that there are four different ways in which individuals learn, and that the learning can be enhanced if the right approach is used for different individuals. David Kolb et al. have developed a model to show how the four types of learning interrelate (figure 7.6).

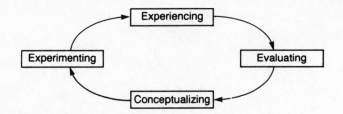

Figure 7.6 The Kolb cycle of learning

Some people learn best by experiencing the task, then evaluating that experience against their previous knowledge. This leads to the development of a concept that experiments with the task can then confirm or deny. Others are happier learning the theory or concepts, experimenting with these, and using the experiences gained to test (evaluate) their concept.

In their *Manual of Learning Styles* Peter Honey and Alan Mumford have looked at which of the Kolb channels (in figure 7.6) different types of people prefer to use to enter the learning cycle. They termed the four types *activists*, *reflectors*, *theorists* and *pragmatists*.

Activists (experiencing)

Activists like new experiences, they enter the cycle at the 'experiences' stage. They are usually willing to try anything and tend to be enthusiastic about new ideas.

They learn best when there are new experiences and problems available, especially where there are short-term results to be gained. They like other people around to bounce ideas off.

They learn least when learning is passive and involves a great deal of reading.

Reflectors (evaluating)

Reflectors like to consider experiences in detail. They tend to be more cautious than activists. Whilst to an Activist the experience is everything and evaluation takes second place, to a Reflector experiences should be short and then there needs to be plenty of time for evaluation.

They learn best when they are encouraged to evaluate an activity and they are given plenty of time to think before going on to the next activity.

They learn least when activity follows activity and they are not given time to consolidate their thoughts.

Theorists (conceptualizing)

Theorists like to integrate their observations and experiences into a logical conceptual framework. They want to know how and why it happened this way. They respond to being given all the details first and then they will try it – the opposite of the Activist, who cannot wait to get his or her hands on the task.

They learn best when they can see how the task fits into the whole and they are directed to the theoretical background to events.

They learn least when they are forced to undertake the task before they have understood the implications and theoretical background.

Pragmatists (experimenting)

Pragmatists want to try out new theoretical ideas in practice: they are experimenters. They tend to be very practical people who can make a link between theory and practice but wish to be sure, via experimentation, that their ideas are correct before undertaking the task proper.

They learn best when they can concentrate on practical issues and they can see the link between theory and practice.

They learn least when they cannot see the relevance between the theory and an immediate practical need.

THINK POINT

- Which is your preferred learning style?
- Have there been occasions when training you have received has been delivered using an inappropriate style for yourself?
- How effective was that training?

A supervisor/FLM who can assess the position of a member of staff within the above categories will be able to target the training entry point at the appropriate Kolb channel, and thus increase the chances of effective learning taking place.

If the member of staff is an Activist, they will not respond to a day of talk and seminars before getting their hands on the task, whereas a Theorist will find this approach effective.

There is a questionnaire in Honey and Mumford that can aid you in assessing your staff if you so wish, although observation of how your staff appear to learn may be enough to allow you to assess an individual's preferred learning style.

If consideration is given to the style best suited to individuals, it is possible, even with a group of staff possessing different learning styles, to devise programmes that meet all needs by ensuring that 'individuals feel comfortable with the training: those who need to read up on it are given opportunities, those who wish to experiment are given the chance etc. When the training is one to one, the supervisor/FLM has an opportunity to tailor the training to the recipient's style and not his or her own.

Case Note 20

Jean was pleased that the Authority had decided that she should gain extra qualifications to go with her new position. She had been enrolled on a 'Certificate in Supervisory Management' programme at her local college.

One of the first sessions concerned learning styles. Jean discovered that she was a Reflector.

'That was useful,' she explained to her tutor after the session. 'I've been trying to explain new procedures to Marcus and all he wants to do is to see the forms and then how we input them into the computers – I think he must be an activist. I'll try the questionnaire we used with some of the other staff. Perhaps we can make our training more effective.'

When members of staff are undertaking training it is imperative that they receive support from their colleagues and their supervisor/line manager. If the training takes them out of the workplace, then they must not feel that others think that they are off having a good time. If staff are being trained, then others may have to pick up a heavier workload, they need to know that they too will receive any necessary training and that they will receive the same support.

Evaluation of training

Training costs time and money and thus it is important that the organization knows that it is receiving value for money. It is also important that those delivering the training can assess their success.

Training should result in a task being carried out more effectively, and it is useful if the supervisor/FLM sets out some aims for the training prior to commencement, such as:

> At the end of this training X will be able to do Y in such and such a time with an accuracy of Z.

In this way the outcomes of training can be measured.

Staff undertaking outside training should be asked to evaluate it and to report back to their supervisor, who can then report to whoever is paying for the training.

When training occurs away from the workplace, the supervisor/FLM should ensure that the benefits of the training reach as many staff as possible by allowing the person receiving the training time to pass on any new knowledge or skills to their colleagues.

Coaching

Whilst the individual supervisor/FLM may not always be involved in the delivery of training, they will be involved in coaching. Training can be equated to the acquiring of a skill, coaching is the process whereby that skill is developed and 'honed' (as such it is a continuing process). The supervisor/FLM is probably the person best placed to deliver coaching; they are on the spot and concerned with the practicalities of the job in hand.

Coaching, like training, is sometimes viewed with a degree of caution. Have I time to coach somebody? Will the process expose my weaknesses? Will they end up so good that they want my job? All of these arguments have been used by individuals as a reason not to coach and train. A moment's reflection will show that they are without valid foundation.

If the supervisor is confident in their job, and if they want the tasks under their control done well, then training and its development through coaching will aid them in their work. Coaching does take time, but it is time that can be recouped through staff being better at their jobs and producing a higher quality product or service.

Appraisal

Appraisal is the process which evaluates a member of staff's performance in the workplace on a formal basis. Not all organizations have an appraisal scheme, and those that are in operation can vary widely.

There are two basic forms of performance appraisal: appraisal linked to pay, and appraisal not linked to pay.

A number or organizations use pay-linked appraisal systems according to which staff are assessed on their past year's performance and awarded increments, or bonus payments, based on whether or not they have achieved the objectives set at their last pay appraisal interview.

Common to all appraisal systems should be a number of basic concepts, concepts that have considerable implications for the supervisor/FLM:

1 Appraisal should commence with an interview with your immediate supervisor/FLM; thus for your staff, you will be the main appraiser; or, if company policy does not use supervisors/FLMs as appraisers, you will be providing much of the information upon which the appraisal is based.
2 Appraisal should be a two-way process: it should be a forum for frank discussion in which both parties can make their feelings known.
3 Appraisal should be concerned with the evaluation of past performance and the setting of future objectives and targets.

An effective appraisal scheme is an on-going process, not a once a year occasion (see figure 7.7).

The appeals procedure is an important part of the appraisal procedure; staff should have the right of appeal to a superior if they disagree with any of the appraiser's comments. In many organizations, the 'Grandfather' is the appraiser's appraiser.

As a supervisor/line manager it is quite likely that you too will be appraised, will have the same rights and follow the same procedures as your staff.

Appraisal interviews are important events and should be prepared for with care. The appraisee should receive plenty of notice before the interview. They should be told what topics are to be discussed and should have a copy of their previous appraisal to hand. The interview itself should be conducted without interruptions, telephones should

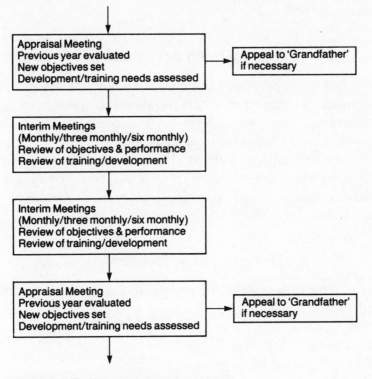

Figure 7.7 The appraisal process

be switched off or calls diverted. The appraisee should be given the opportunity to place items on the agenda.

The aim of the interview should be to review performance and to see how any shortcomings, if any, can be rectified. The appraisal interview should not be an opportunity for the supervisor/FLM to 'have a go' at an employee without warning. If this happens it could be asked why the matter had to wait for an appraisal interview before being raised.

The interview should produce a new set of objectives for the next period together with agreement on any training or development needed to help fulfil those objectives. The aim should be to arrive at a consensus that the employee feels they can 'own', for in this way appraisal can help serve both individual and organizational development.

A written record should be kept of actions and objectives agreed, this document forming the basis of the next appraisal. Interim meetings can be held between appraisals in order to monitor progress and development.

Management development

Not only has the supervisor/FLM a responsibility for the training and development of their staff, there is also a responsibility for the development of their own supervisory/management skills – indeed, this is what the *In Charge* series is all about.

The interested supervisor/FLM should discuss their management development with their manager or their personnel/training department to ascertain the most appropriate programme for the organization and themselves.

Resignation or Retirement

Sooner or later people leave the organization for one of a number of reasons:

- They obtain a job elsewhere
- They are dismissed
- They leave for personal or domestic reasons
- The job is made redundant and they are paid off
- They retire either at retirement age or through ill health (this includes death)

Where people leave for other posts it is worth conducting an *exit interview* to see if you can find out their reasons for leaving. In many cases it will be for more money, but it may be because they were unhappy with working conditions, or they felt they were not appreciated, or that their prospects did not match their ambitions. People may be reluctant to give their true reasons for leaving, but it is worth trying to find them out.

Whenever somebody retires or leaves to have a family etc., it may be worth staying in touch – not only do they leave but they take their skills, experience and contacts with them. They may be willing to assist the organization from time to time, and the supervisor/FLM is well placed to act as a link and a point of contact.

When somebody leaves, this provides an opportunity to re-evaluate the job as discussed at the beginning of the last chapter.

SUMMARY

Supervisory Management Standards:

Unit C9   Contribute to the development of teams and individuals
          OPTIONAL for VQ Level 3
Unit C12 (part of)
          Lead the work of teams and individuals to achieve their objectives
          OPTIONAL for VQ Level 3

Element C9.1   Contribute to the identification of development needs
         C9.2   Contribute to planning the development of teams and
                individuals
         C9.3   Contribute to development activities
         C9.4   Contribute to the assessment of people against
                development objectives
         C12.3 Provide feedback to teams and individuals on their work

The Management Standards make quite clear of the need for supervisors/FLMs to contribute to the training, coaching and appraising of staff.

Induction is a key process in achieving an effective workforce, and the contribution and commitment of the supervisor to the process is crucial.

The 'employment cycle' was continued after appointment and includes induction, training and appraisal. The latter process has an important role in the setting of objectives and letting staff know how they are doing.

Staff use different learning styles and a knowledge of these allows the supervisor/FLM to make training more effective.

RECOMMENDED FURTHER READING

G. A. Cole, *Personnel Management, Theory and Practice* (1988), chapters 22–30.

Chapter 8

Groups and Teams

Case Note 21

'Now we've appointed the staff, we can work on making them an effective team, don't you agree Jean?' asked Mr Rawlings one afternoon.

Of course Jean agreed, but she wasn't very sure what he meant. How did you make an effective team? And which teams should she concentrate on? There seemed to be about five different teams reporting to her: were they separate teams or were they all part of a bigger team . . . and what was the difference between a group and a team?

This chapter is about the supervision/first line management (FLM) of groups and teams.

The study of how group behaviour differs from that of individuals is a very interesting one, and the chapter begins by looking at how writers on behaviour have sought to define what a group is and why one should study it. You need not remember the names of all the writers in this field, but it is interesting and useful to consider the different definitions they have produced.

WHY STUDY GROUPS?

The management theories of the classical school of Taylor and others (chapter 4) proposed that the relationship between employee and manager or supervisor was one based on economics and individuality. This concept equates to Schein's idea of 'economic man', one of four possible categories relating to motivation and work proposed by Schein in the 1980s. The other three categories were: 'social man', 'self-actualizing man' and 'complex man'. Economic man related to the possible motivation caused by money, self-actualizing man wished to achieve his or her potential, social man was an attempt to explain our social and belonging needs, and complex man was an amalgam of the other three. Schein's work was an attempt to undo the simplification of Taylor and workers like McGregor who had postulated two sets of presumptions about people in organizations, viz. Theory X and Theory Y. Theory X has a great deal in common with Taylor's views about employees, but both ideas ignore the social needs of the individual. It was the work of Mayo and his associates at the Hawthorn Plant of General Electric, which showed that other factors beside economic ones are at work within organizations, and play a considerable role in both motivation and effectiveness.

The findings of the Mayo study as regards the study of groups and teams can be summarized as follows:

- Groups serve both the needs of the organization and the individual.
- Most groups have both formal and informal functions.
- One of the important facts about groups in the organizational context rests on the ability of their members to unite against management and frustrate their policies. (This rather negative aspect of group dynamics was a direct finding of the study and needs to be borne in mind by the supervisor/FLM as one of the downsides of working with groups.)
- The informal functions and norms (rules) may go counter to the formal functions and norms (rules).

- The satisfaction that an individual gains from group membership may constitute a more potent reward than management can offer;
- Individuals may thus be subjected to conflicting motivational forces.
- Group unity and solidarity is also a means to force management to improve a group's rewards.

DEFINITIONS OF GROUPS

THINK POINT

Consider a queue waiting for a bus and one of your teams at work. In general terms we could use the word 'group' to describe both of them; how do they differ?

In defining the concept of a 'group' in work and social terms, a number of different approaches have been adopted. As stated earlier, you do not need to remember the names of all the workers who have produced the definitions and ideas, but it is worth you considering each one carefully to see how different approaches can be applied to the same concept.

Homans (1950) considered that:

We mean by a group, a number of persons who communicate with one another, often over a span of time, and who are few enough so that each person is able to communicate with all the others, not at second hand through others, but face to face.

This, rather tight, definition would seem to exclude groups such as teachers, police officers, or the staff of a large company by virtue of size.

Fiedler (1964) saw groups in terms of *interdependency*:

By this term [group] we generally mean a set of individuals who share a common fate, that is, who are interdependent in the sense that an event that affects one member is likely to affect all others.

This definition is more useful when considering the behaviour of professional/occupational groups, as it is less dependent upon face-to-face contact.

Some writers consider that a collection of people can only be considered as a group if they have *common identifiable goals*. Deutsch, writing in 1949, stated:

A psychological group exists (has unity) to the extent that the individuals composing it perceive themselves as pursuing promotively interdependent goals.

Motivation and *need satisfaction* are considered by some to be the main criteria for the definition of a group. Cattell's (1951) definition was:

The definition which seems most essential is that a group is a collection of organisms in which the existence of all (in their given relationships) is necessary to the satisfaction of certain individual needs in each.

Sherif and Sherif (1956), who carried out many experiments on group behaviour, considered groups in terms of *social relationships* with a clear set of role definitions and norms. Their definition of a group was:

a social unit which consists of a number of individuals who stand in (more or less) definite status and role relationships to one another and which possesses a set of values and norms of its own regulating the behaviour of individual members, at least in matters of consequence to the group.

Shaw (1976) defined a group as 'two or more persons who are interacting with each other in such a manner that each person influences and is influenced by each other person.'

Running through the work of all the above is the concept of 'perceptions of membership'. If the members do not perceive themselves to be a group, then they will be less likely to behave as a group.

For the purposes of considering workgroups and teams, a useful definition combining the ideas quoted above is this:

A group in the context of occupation or profession, is a collection of individuals operating within the constraints of mutually accepted norms (rules) and values who perceive that, as regards their occupation or profession, they are clearly distinct from other collections of individuals even if they belong to the same organization.

A group at work may have both organizational and professional loyalties. The definition above allows both of these to be addressed by recognizing the wider implications of membership of a professional group which crosses geographic and organizational boundaries. A person may be a member of the personnel department at work, but also a member of the Institute of Personnel Managers, with its own code of professional conduct. Conflicts can occur between the two.

The above definition allows individuals to belong to a whole series of groups, adopting the norms and values prevalent with the group they are identifying with at the moment in question. This is a similar concept to the 'language registers' proposed by Bernstein (1961). Bernstein considered that an individual's use of language was dependent upon the circumstances and that we all have a series of different language registers, one for home, one for work (e.g. technical terminology), one for friends etc. Similarly we may have a wide variety of norms and values to draw upon, within our basic cultural norms, and we can switch from group to group.

THINK POINT

Do you use different language (words, phrases and even accents) when you are at work, out socially or at home? In what ways are they different?

GROUP DYNAMICS

Between the wars, and especially following the conclusion of World War Two, a considerable degree of research was undertaken into the difference between group behaviour and that of individuals. A new vocabulary grew up related to ideas of 'group dynamics'. Researchers looked at the advantages and disadvantages of working in groups and a set of clear ideas began to form. Sherif (1936) was one of the first to use the concept of social control through group norms. His experiments used moving lights in dark rooms to produce an autokinetic effect, and showed how individual perceptions were modified by other members of the group so as to produce a group result: i.e., members of the group saw a light moving in the same way despite differences in vision and perception. Following on from Mayo's work cited earlier, Roethlisberger and Dickson (1964) concluded after studying a series of work groups that deviance by individuals was carefully regulated by the group:

> The mechanisms by which internal control was exercised varied. Perhaps the most important were sarcasm . . . and ridicule. Through such devices pressure was brought to bear upon those individuals who deviated from the group's norm of acceptable conduct.

The ease with which a group is able to obtain conformity from its members can of course be of considerable disadvantage. Asch's (1951) experiments – in which participants appeared willing to back incorrect statements which emanated from the group, especially when the individual perceived themselves to be of lower status – highlighted the strength of adherence to group norms.

Yablonsky's study of street gangs in Chicago showed how clearly the power of the group manifests itself. He found that adherence to the gang's norms could easily transcend other accepted societal norms, that the leader's commands sometimes were obeyed even when these conflicted with the law, and that fear of retribution from other gang members, especially in the form of rejection, could easily produce aberrant behaviour.

That human beings are social animals and are thus subject to group as opposed to personal pressures has long been known. It was the Count Cavour writing in the last century who said: 'What scoundrels we would be if we did for ourselves what we do for Italy'. Such an excuse has been used by war criminals ever since; we were not acting for ourselves but for the group. Morris, Lorenz and Ardrey in the 1960s looked at animal, and especially primate, societies and concluded that group dynamics may have its roots in primate evolution.

Given that the group 'instinct' is so strong within primates (and man is a primate in biological terms), it is of little surprise that it has become the subject of considerable interest in regard to the study of human behaviour conducted in the fields of psychology, sociology and organizational behaviour.

The post World War Two studies of groups have shown that groups are far more prone to risk-taking than individuals. This can be both an advantage and a disadvantage. In a fast-moving business environment, an increased propensity to take risks may give an organization a considerable strategic advantage. The success of many Japanese businesses after the war has been attributed in part to their willingness to experiment and take risks compared with their Western competitors.

Taking risks can be an advantage or a disadvantage: if the decision and course of action are correct, then risk-taking is an advantage that groups have over individuals. Group membership allows the risks and any consequent blame to be spread amongst the members. If a scapegoat is sought, it is often somebody outside the immediate group.

THINK POINT

Can you think of any group decisions that you have been involved with that you would have considered too risky if you had had to make them in isolation?

GROUP THINK

The American researcher Janis coined the phrase 'Group Think' in 1968 after studying a number of US foreign policy disasters. Groups can spread the risk (and guilt) amongst members, thus diluting the individual's responsibility. This has long been observed but has never been accepted in law; the Nuremberg Trials after 1945 are a classic example. There is also the considerable body of research quoted earlier which shows that individuals find non-conformity with the group view difficult. Tice (1989) in his seminars, written supporting materials, and audio and video presentations for the Pacific Institute, makes great play on the role of individual accountability within a group organizational context, but concedes that group pressure can sometimes be impossible to withstand. Couple this with risk-taking and the concept of 'group invulnerability' expounded by Janis (1968), and a wrong decision becomes a recipe for potential disaster, and possibly war.

Case Note 22

Jean left the inter-departmental meeting in an unhappy frame of mind. Sitting with colleagues in the canteen later she remarked, 'I'm sorry, I know I didn't say anything, but I really didn't agree with the final decision.'

'To tell you you the truth, neither did I,' said Simon.

'Nor I,' replied three other voices almost in unison.

'Then why didn't we say something?' asked Jean.

'I thought everybody else was happy, so I didn't want to rock the boat or look stupid,' answered Simon.

A classic example of Group Think in action: nobody appeared to agree with the decision, but nobody said anything because they thought that everybody else was happy!

THINK POINT

Can you think of any occasions when you have been affected by Group Think? Have you been prepared to speak up in a minority?

TEAMS

A team is a small group, usually formed for a specific set of tasks. Its members will normally be well known to each other and it can be thought of as a 'focused group'. It is the commonality of the task, rather than membership or in some cases size, that defines the difference between organization, group and team. An example can be found in a football club.

The club is the organization and it comprises several groups, all with objectives that enable the club to fulfil its aims: making a profit, being successful, being part of the community etc. There are a number of groups: directors, groundstaff, administrators, players. Within these groups there will be teams; one team is obvious, it is the one that goes out each Saturday to play, but there will also be a wages team, a fanclub team and so on. Membership of these teams will change from time to time, but the members will come from the group. People may also be members of more than one team: a player might also be part of the press team, for example.

THE CONCEPT OF SYNERGY

If 'Group Think' can be avoided, the concept of *synergy*, whereby the sum of the parts exceeds the whole, can play a vital role in making groups more effective than individuals. Studies on effective group work show that synergy works to increase effectiveness over that expected in certain groups, but in others leads to a decrease in efficiency over that predicted in others.

A well-constructed and well-managed team is capable of producing better results than might have been predicted by looking at the capabilities of the individual members. A badly constructed and/or badly managed team may well not fulfil its potential. The FA Cup produces a number of 'giant-killers' each year, lower division teams or even amateurs that defeat teams costing millions of pounds to assemble. Synergy may provide part of the answer to this phenomenon.

Synergy, like risk-taking, is a two-edged sword; in well-constructed teams the characteristics of synergy lead to improved performance whilst in teams that are less well constructed they lead to decreased performance. The construction of effective teams is discussed later in this chapter with an examination of the work of Meredith Belbin.

GROUP NORMS

Groups set their own rules. These are often called 'group norms'. This can be a considerable advantage when it comes to groups in the workplace. The group will set rules about breaks etc. and can be self-policing. A group knows the standards for work rate and production and can assist in ensuring that any slackness is rectified. On the other hand, Mayo's experiments, as described in Buchanan and Huczynski (1985), showed that the group would also act to bring down the work rate of a high-performing individual to that of the agreed 'norm' for the group – as was said earlier, the use of groups can be a two-edged sword.

THINK POINT

Think of the groups in your work situation.
- Can you see examples of group norms in operation?
- Do the group norms conflict with or complement management rules?

Case Note 23

Jean was chairing a team meeting. She had decided to allow her team of senior staff to examine the working patterns and rotas.

The procedures they had developed seemed sensible, so she decided to let them be put into operation for a trial one-month period. She was especially interested to see if their ideas about flexible working (staff working for any eight hours between 8 a.m. and 6 p.m.) would be practical, as one of her predecessors had tried to implement such a scheme and it had not worked very well because nobody wanted early and late turns.

At the end of the month she was amazed at the success – there had been few problems and the work group sorted those that had occurred themselves. She mentioned this to Mr Rawlings.

'I'm not surprised,' he commented; 'It was their scheme after all, they had ownership of it, so as a group they became responsible for making it work.'

GROUP EVOLUTION

Groups and teams do not occur as fully formed entities any more than adult humans do; like us, they go through a period of growth and evolution. There were originally thought to be four stages in group and team evolution, but the present authors take the view that there actually are five. The original four are discussed below.

Forming

When a group or team is first formed, the initial task is to get to know each other. This is the most social phase of group/team evolution. Very little productive work occurs; the members are, perhaps, still slightly wary of each other, as people may not know the skills and capabilities of one another. They are normally fairly polite and formal in communications.

If we were to consider the *forming* stage on a diagram of productivity against time it would look like figure 8.1. Such a situation cannot last; nor, given the relatively low productivity, should it. The next stage is less comfortable.

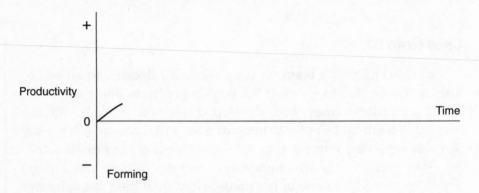

Figure 8.1 Group/team evolution: 'forming'

Storming

We all have our own personal objectives for membership of a group; what we want to obtain from what the group does might not coincide with what other members want. The group might agree procedures that we do not like, or we might be unhappy with the tasks we are allocated or the time we are required to give, or even with the way we are treated.

Sooner or later something has to be said. A person might find they are on their own in their concerns, or they may find that others agree with them and are relieved that the matter has been raised – remember Group Think. This may cause a degree of dissension and harsh words may be said; it does not mean that the group is splitting up, rather that a natural evolution is occurring. The process of members making their feelings known is called *storming* and is a natural part of group/team evolution. It is not necessarily a violent conflict and people do not have to run around becoming agitated, although this can happen, but they will want to air their views about the way the group is run. The task of the supervisor/FLM is to manage this situation and not to let it get out of hand by becoming too personal or disruptive. It should not be avoided or suppressed, else the next stage of group/team evolution may be delayed. If people do not have their say, they will become resentful and productivity may suffer even more. During storming, productivity will dip and may even become negative for a short time (worry etc. can cause mistakes). Storming is shown in figure 8.2.

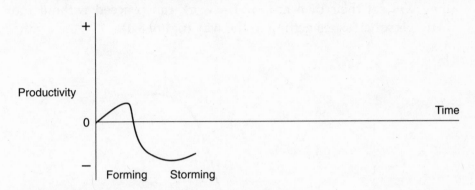

Figure 8.2 Group/team evolution: 'storming'

Norming

Once storming has brought things out into the open, a process of setting the group/team rules can begin in earnest. Members can decide who is doing what, when they are doing it, to what standard and what the reporting procedures will be. Housekeeping issues such as meal breaks, smoking policy etc. can be agreed – with these decided the group/team is ready to go to work. Productivity begins to increase, as shown in figure 8.3.

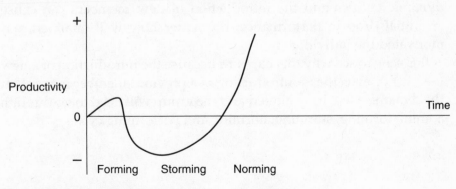

Figure 8.3 Group/team evolution: 'norming'

Performing

Performing is what the group/team was set up to do, but it has had to go through the forming, storming and norming stages, to a greater or lesser degree first. Once the group/team has set its norms – and it is best that they set them rather than having them imposed from above (they will set their own anyway) – work can proceed without too many personal issues getting in the way (figure 8.4).

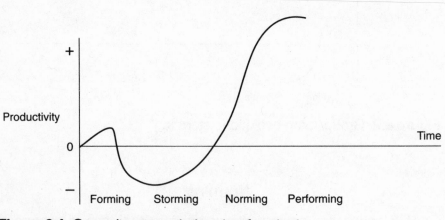

Figure 8.4 Group/team evolution: 'performing'

Reforming

Many books on supervision and management cover the forming, storming, norming and performing stages but groups and teams are dynamic entities and the introduction of new members can cause an initial drop in performance, no matter how well qualified and motivated the individual is.

It is easy to see why this happens because the introduction of a new member or even the re-introduction of a previous member means that the dynamics will have altered and the group will need to go through a 'mini' forming, storming, norming and performing cycle.

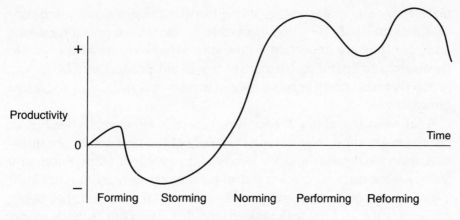

Productivity

Forming   Storming   Norming   Performing   Reforming

Figure 8.5 Group/team evolution: 'reforming'

THINK POINT

'It must be that new lad,' said one of Jean's staff one morning; 'That team worked perfectly well together before he was trans- ferred to them, we never had any problem. Move him out and everything will be fine.'

What advice would you give Jean? Have you ever been in the situation where a new member seems to have a very detrimental effect on a previously productive group/team – how was the situation handled?

The introduction of a new member to a group/team may mean that the whole evolution process needs to start again – new relationships may require new norms. Families see this when there is a new baby in the house.

THE SOCIAL ASPECTS OF GROUPS

In addition to the task, groups/teams need some time to act in a social manner. Time needs to be available for group relationships to be strengthened and for informal storming and norming to occur. Coffee breaks, meal times, social events all provide opportunities for 'group maintenance activities', times when the group looks inward and concentrates on itself. They do not need to be formalized or last for a long time, but they are important – give your groups/teams a little time to themselves to spend as they wish; it will aid productivity because a group that has strong bonds between members is usually a productive group.

Adair, writing about leadership, saw the effective leadership of groups as a compromise among the needs of the task and/or organization, individual needs and the needs of the group or team. Successful leaders were ones who managed to balance these needs so that individuals were motivated, group needs for social cohesion, belonging etc. were met, and the task was effectively carried out. Adair's model is represented in figure 8.6.

Figure 8.6 The Adair leadership model

THINK POINT

How often do the groups you belong to or supervise have an opportunity to act in a social rather than a task role?

Hastings et al. (1986), of the Ashridge Group in the UK, looked at the factors leading to group success and concluded that there were a whole series of concepts relating to planning, motivating and leadership required within the team, that great care needed to be taken of the team as opposed to functional roles undertaken by members, that different mechanisms were needed to deal with geographically dispersed groups, and that the role and commitment of the outside sponsor was critical to success.

Buchanan and Huczynski (1985), in considering this problem of large, dispersed groups, conclude that the 'shared frame of reference' concept is of vital importance:

> A 'frame of reference' is the assumption that we make about the kind of situations we are confronting. It is the context within which we view it. A frame of reference which is shared by the members of the group means that through their interaction and mutual education, the members of this group will tend to perceive a large range of phenomena in broadly the same way.

Frames of reference are formed through common experiences, culture, education and so forth; the more coherent a group, the more likely it is that the members of it will make the same assumptions and have the same perceptions when they are given the same information.

Even if somebody is working away from the group/team the supervisor/FLM should ensure that they still feel that they belong and that every effort is made to keep them informed.

THE CONCEPT OF TEAM ROLES

Buchanan and Huczynski considered that the structure of a group can be differentiated in the following ways: liking, status, power, leadership and role. It is on the latter that the next section of this chapter centres. They also noted the fact that most people have in fact two roles within a group: the role they perceive that they should have and the role that they actually enact. Belbin's work (1981), which is discussed next, attempts to encourage convergence between the two, and also looks at the difference between the functional role within a group that members are allocated and the more personality-based team role that they adopt naturally.

Team roles are described by Belbin as:

> a pattern of behaviour characteristic of the way in which one team member interacts with another where his performance serves to facilitate the progress of the team as a whole.

The work of Meredith Belbin, initially at the Henley Management Centre and later in Cambridge, has provided a clearer insight into internal group relationships and clarified the roles needed for a team or group to work effectively.

Belbin suggests that there are nine possible team roles that a person can adopt. Some are natural roles, some are roles that a person can adopt if necessary, and some are roles that the person finds very hard to adopt. Other work, such as that carried out by Margerison and McCann (1985), has come up with very similar findings. The team types Belbin postulated are:

Plant (PL):	Very creative, the ideas person
Resource Investigator (RI):	Extrovert, good at making outside contacts and developing ideas
Monitor–evaluator (ME):	Shrewd and prudent: analytical
Shaper (SH):	Dynamic and challenging
Coordinator (CO):	Respected, mature and good at ensuring that talents are used effectively
Implementor (IMP):	Practical, loyal and task orientated
Completer–finisher (CF):	Meticulous and attentive to detail
Teamworker (TW):	Caring and very person oriented
Specialist (SP):	High technical skill; professional as opposed to organizational prime loyalties

Margerison and McCann (1985) saw roles in terms of those who were most happily suited to: innovating, promoting, developing, organizing, producing, inspecting, maintaining and advising. These roles can easily be correlated with the Belbin roles as follows:

Belbin	*Margerison et al.*
Plant	Innovating/promoting
Resource investigator	Promoting/developing
Monitor–evaluator	Inspecting/advising
Shaper	Maintaining/developing
Coordinator	Organizing
Completer–finisher	Inspecting
Implementor	Producing
Team worker	Maintaining

For each of the team role 'strengths' quoted above, Belbin considered that there were allowable weaknesses, the price that had to be paid for the strength.

The allowable weakness postulated by Belbin are:

Plant (PL):	Weak in communicating with and managing ordinary people
Resource Investigator (RI):	Easily bored after the initial enthusiasm has passed
Monitor–Evaluator (ME):	Lacks drive and ability to inspire others
Shaper (SH):	Prone to provocation and bursts of temper
Coordinator (CO):	Not necessarily the most clever or creative member of the group
Implementor (IMP):	Inflexible and slow to respond to new opportunities
Completer–finisher (CF):	Inclined to worry and reluctant to delegate
Teamworker (TW):	Indecisive in crunch situations
Specialist (SP):	Contributes on only a narrow front

It is dangerous to treat the allowable weaknesses as areas to be removed; to do so might also involve losing the underlying strength. Rather, they need to be managed and understood.

Research using the Belbin concepts has shown that having a language to describe strengths and weaknesses in this way allows group/team members to understand each other and aids the work process.

THINK POINT

What do you believe are your preferred team roles? How well balanced is your team – are there any gaps that need filling?
Consider the members of your workgoup/team. Which are their preferred team roles and which roles should they avoid?
Think about famous people: what roles did they prefer? Make a list. Here are some ideas to start you off:

Plant	Clive Sinclair
Shaper	Margaret Thatcher
Coordinator	George Bush

All those who have written on teamwork have stressed the need for a balance or blend of team members. Belbin himself stresses the need for balance and this is echoed by writers such as McGregor (1960), who wrote of the need for a balance of roles within managerial teams. McGregor was concerned that the creative (*plant* in Belbin terms) and dynamic (*shaper* in Belbin terms) roles should be counterbalanced by a critical thinking (*monitor–evaluator* in Belbin terms) role within the team. In order to test for team role types, Belbin developed the '*interplace*' computer program, which produces a profile and a series of reports. Interplace is marketed as a recruitment aid, as are other tests (e.g., 16PF and OPQ) which use similar terms to describe team roles. Belbin's research showed that effective teams were comprised of between 5–7 members and contained a blend of team role types. As there are 9 team role types, people need to use more than one type: i.e., a person may act as a *plant* at the beginning of a project but as a *specialist* later on etc. Teams containing members who all had high team role scores (Apollo Teams) were not especially effective, and teams containing only 2 or 3 roles were very ineffective. A team of *plants* might be very creative but would be unlikely to implement the ideas while, conversely, a team of *implementors* might be very practical but would lack the creativity to break new ground.

In his original work, Belbin used the term 'chairman' (CH) instead of *coordinator* and 'company worker' (CW) instead of *implementor*. The role of *specialist* is a later addition and does not figure in the original research.

Generalizing about team roles, Buchanan and Huczynski split them up into two main sections, task roles and maintenance roles. The task roles are: initiator, information seeker, diagnoser, opinion seeker, evaluator, decision manager. The maintenance functions are: encourager, compromiser, peacekeeper, clarifier, summarizer, standard setter. These categories can easily be equated with the Belbin team roles. If certain team roles predominate in a particular professional/occupational group, then there is the danger that any team formed from members of that group will not function as effectively as possible. Eleven centre forwards may have considerable collective talent but are unlikely to perform as well as a team containing a goalkeeper, defenders, middle players etc. Similarly, a workteam with too many *plants* may produce too many conflicting ideas with a lack of follow through.

When recruiting new members to a group/team, the supervisor/ FLM should consider not only the tasks that the person will be carrying out but also the roles present within the group/team and the type of roles the applicant has as natural roles. Whilst software such as *interplace* is very useful, careful questioning and observation can allow an objective assessment of an applicant's preferred team role to be made. The aim should be to seek a balanced group/team, both in terms of functional and team roles.

Case Note 24

Jean was looking at the results of Belbin team profiling Ayesha had carried out for her on the members of the section.

'That explains a lot,' she remarked. 'I've had somebody who appears to be a completer–finisher, and she is very meticulous you know, trying to come up with ideas for the new office layout, and I've been using my most creative person on filing. I think I'll swap them round.'

'A good idea,' replied Ayesha, 'and make sure that you listen to your monitor–evaluator – they may throw a damper on things but a good monitor–evaluator is seldom wrong.'

SUMMARY

Supervisory Management Standards:

Unit C7   Contribute to the selection of personnel for activities
OPTIONAL for VQ Level 3

Element C7.2   Contribute to selecting required personnel

Unit C9   Contribute to the development of teams and individuals
OPTIONAL for VQ Level 3
Unit C12 (part of)
Lead the work of teams and individuals to achieve their objectives
OPTIONAL for VQ Level 3

Element C9.1   Contribute to the identification of development needs
C9.2   Contribute to planning the development of teams and individuals
C9.3   Contribute to development activities
C9.4   Contribute to the assessment of people against development activities
C12.3 Provide feedback to teams and individuals on their work

People do not work on their own; most people are members of various groups and teams, a team being a focused group.

There are advantages and disadvantages of working in groups and teams relating to the ideas of synergy, risk taking and 'Group Think'. The competent supervisor/FLM needs to be aware of these advantages and disadvantages.

Groups evolve through a process of *forming*, *storming*, *norming* and *performing*, eventually decaying. This evolution has implications for the formation and continuance of work groups.

Belbin's work considers the team roles people fulfil in addition to the functional role as laid out in their job description. He describes nine basic team roles. An effective team is composed of a balance of individuals, chosen for both functional and team roles, this having a major implication for recruitment.

RECOMMENDED FURTHER READING

Meredith Belbin, *Management Teams, Why They Succeed or Fail* (1981).
Colin Hastings et al. *Superteams* (1986).
David and Frank Johnson, *Joining Together, Group Theory and Group Skills*

Chapter 9

The Supervisor/ First Line Manager as a Leader

Supervisory Management Standards:

Unit C4   Create effective working relationships
           MANDATORY for VQ Level 3

Unit C15 Create effective working relationships
           OPTIONAL for VQ Level 3

Element   C4.1   Gain the trust and support of colleagues and
                 team members
          C4.3   Minimise conflict in your team

Element   C15.1 Help team members who have problems
                 affecting their performance

This chapter of *Managing People* examines the leadership role of the supervisor/first line manager (FLM). As a supervisor/FLM you may not feel that you are a leader as such, but as far as your team and your subordinates are concerned this may be one of their perceptions of you.

Case Note 25

'We need to do something,' Adrian said to the meeting in general. 'The new canteen arrangements are completely unacceptable and the prices are far too high for the standard of food.'

There was general agreement from all of Jean's staff.

'I agree,' she said. 'But what can we do? It's all been decided.'

'Well,' replied Adrian, 'you're supposed to be the leader of this section, if our leader can't or won't do anything it's a poor lookout for the rest of us.'

It is unlikely that the supervisor/FLM will have the term 'leader' in their job description and it is unlikely that they will expect to be a leader in the classical sense of the word: supervisors/FLMs are not expected to ride out, on a white charger, at the head of their troops, but they are expected to fulfil a leadership role.

This leadership role involves motivating, challenging, developing, supporting, disciplining (where necessary) and inspiring their subordinates. They will be expected to behave in a manner appropriate to that of a leader.

THINK POINT

What do you believe are the types of behaviour that a person in a leadership role should display?

You may well have answered that the leadership role should involve attributes such as: honesty, integrity, supportiveness, a willingness to delegate, and a thorough knowledge of the task and the organization.

This chapter examines the leadership role of the supervisor/FLM by looking at the way in which he or she:

- Coordinates the activities of a team
- Motivates and supports staff
- Exercises power and influence
- Delegates
- Develops and challenges

The chapter commences with a consideration of how thinking about the leadership role has developed and the characteristics of different leadership styles, styles you will probably recognize from your knowledge of the world or your experiences at work.

THINK POINT

Do you think that leadership is something that a person is born with or is it something that can be learned, practised and developed?

This is a question that many of those concerned with management development and organizational behaviour have considered. The general opinion seems to be that whilst there appear to be certain 'leadership' traits, many of the factors that enable a person to exercise a leadership role can be developed.

LEADERSHIP v MANAGEMENT – IS THERE A DIFFERENCE?

In chapter 4 we considered two definitions of management:

> To manage is to forecast and plan, to organize, to command, to coordinate and to control. (Fayol)

> The five essential managerial functions are: planning, organizing, staffing, directing and leading and controlling. (Koontz and O'Donnell)

Fayol speaks of 'controlling and commanding', Koontz and O'Donnell of 'directing, leading and controlling'. If we think carefully about these particular supervisory/managerial functions they are those concerned with the exercise of power, responsibility and accountability, areas that form the leadership functions of the supervisor/FLM's role.

THINK POINT

Think about leaders you have met or heard about. Who are they and do they have traits in common, or are there major differences?

One of the attributes that distinguishes leaders is that they serve as a model for others, they are people we wish to emulate, be they national, religious, educational (the teacher you remember most) or vocational (the boss who you would do anything for). Who we would wish to follow and who we consider as a good leader may depend on upbringing, culture, religion, political beliefs etc. One person's great leader is another one's tyrant!

Case Note 26

Jean and three of her subordinates attended a meeting led by the Chief Executive.

'He's good isn't he?' said one of her colleagues. 'I don't know what it is, but you really can listen to him – he seems to care.'

'Good leaders do care, or at least, in a real world, appear to care,' thought Jean; 'I wonder whether my staff feel that I'm a natural leader? I know I don't.'

It appears to be quite difficult to suggest an exhaustive list of traits for good leaders, since every survey seems to add new traits to the list, but in general we can conclude that a good leader needs to have developed the majority of the following traits:

- honesty
- integrity
- fairness
- good at communicating
- people skills
- vision
- ability to make difficult decisions
- smart appearance
- confidence
- intelligence

By intelligence it is not implied that a leader needs to be extraordinarily clever, but rather that they need to possess above average common sense and perhaps a degree of manipulative ability.

THINK POINT

How do you rate yourself on the above qualities?

Power

If power is a factor in leadership, we need to consider what power is. Power is a very emotive subject and often conjures up negative images. In a supervisory/managerial sense power is neither positive nor negative; it is simply a resource that A uses to influence B in order to obtain a desired result.

There are a number of sources of power that a supervisor/FLM can use. Whilst power itself may be neutral, how it is employed may be viewed as positive or negative according to the situation.

The principle sources of power are:

Physical

Hopefully the supervisor/FLM will not have to use any physical power to fulfil their duties. Discussions amongst supervisors within the armed forces, the emergency services and even within hospitals suggest that there are occasions when the threat of physical force, or an ability to respond to somebody's use of force, may be necessary.

Whilst it would not be the norm for a supervisor/FLM to use physical power, he or she may face the threat of it being used against them. Physical power is the most primitive of the power sources; and some members of society are more ready to use it than others.

Position

In a hierarchy, a person's position gives them power because of the perceptions that others have of the power that goes with the job.

Within any organization, people do things that they are told because of the position of the person telling them. The newly appointed supervisor/FLM will find that people will do things for them which they might not have been prepared to do previously, because they are a supervisor/FLM.

Resource

Case Note 27

'Ian wants this done today, but it's not one of our priorities. I've no choice, though, as he controls most of the information technology budget and we need that new equipment,' Jean remarked to her staff.

Deliberately or not, Ian was using 'resource power'. If you control resources, you have power at your disposal; whether you use it positively or negatively is your decision. Even supervisors/FLMs quite low down in the hierarchy can possess resource power.

Expert

Even where a person does not control many actual resources they may be able to exert power by nature of their expertise; this is 'expert power'. As a form of power it was much in evidence at the start of computerization in many organizations. Young men and women, junior in terms of position but with a considerable knowledge of the subject, were able to wield considerable power and influence because they possessed the skills to accomplish the tasks that their superiors required.

Personal

A minority of people wield power because of their personality. We would follow them anywhere because of who they are.

THINK POINT

Which sources of power do you find you use most often? Do you use them all or just one or two?

Four concepts that need to be linked to power are: authority, accountability, responsibility and delegation.

Authority can be described as the use of legitimate power. A possesses authority when B recognizes A's right to exert power over B. Power does not have to carry authority with it, but legitimate power is less likely to be challenged. One is less likely to challenge a police officer if stopped in the street than a stranger in civilian clothes. A police officer possesses authority to go with his or her power.

Accountability is the obligation to carry out certain tasks for the organization; accountability is the requirement to ensure that the required tasks are carried out; and delegation is the process of passing on responsibility but retaining accountability.

Accountability means that the person holding that accountability may not necessarily carry out the task but that their responsibility is for ensuring that it is carried out. They are responsible for ensuring that the person carrying out the task knows what they are doing and that they have the necessary resources. If things go wrong, the ultimate responsibility lies with the person who holds the accountability.

Responsibility is concerned with the actual carrying out of the task. The parameters and constraints on the task will be made known and the person to whom responsibility has been given is then expected to carry it out.

Delegation occurs when the person holding accountability for the task passes the responsibility for carrying it out to another. They should also ensure that their authority and any resources required are passed on.

Supervisors/FLMs, and indeed managers in general, often have problems in delegating. One cannot delegate accountability, and so it sometimes seems easier to do the task yourself rather than to delegate it, risk it going wrong and then have to take the blame.

Delegation requires a trust in one's subordinates. If this can be achieved it frees the supervisor/FLM for more important tasks and it acts as a motivator to the subordinate because it both serves as a means of demonstrating trust and developing that subordinate. The supervisor/FLM should not delegate just the unpleasant jobs, and they must be prepared to acknowledge the combinations of the subordinate if praise is being given out. It is also important that, having delegated a task, the supervisor/line manager adopts a hands off approach – lets the subordinate have regular reporting lines and access to resources but does not spend a great deal of time looking over their shoulder. Once a task has been delegated, apart from the accountability it is owned by the subordinate.

Case Note 28

'Don't you trust me completely, Jean?' Adrian asked one morning, 'You asked me to draw up next month's schedules, we discussed them, and I've come in today to find that you've altered them and you didn't even tell me.'

'I'm sorry, but I only did it last night and I am responsible for those schedules. I've every right to amend them,' she replied.

'No,' argued Adrian, clearly upset. 'You have to make sure that they are drawn up but you made me responsible for doing it; I think that we should have discussed it before any changes were made. If I'm not trusted I don't see why I should bother taking responsibility for the schedules – you do it if you want!' and he stormed out.

Jean was clearly upset and angry – for a while. As she thought about the incident, however, she reflected that Adrian was right, and that if she was going to delegate she had to do it properly and not interfere, though she would still need to monitor and evaluate, as one can only delegate responsibility, and not acccountability.

TYPES OF LEADER

There appear to be a number of different types of leader, distinguished not by the style of leadership they adopt (we shall consider styles later), but rather by the mechanism by which they became a leader and to some extent the types of power they use. These are:

Charismatic leaders

Charismatic leaders are leaders because of their personalities. Examples are John F. Kennedy, Margaret Thatcher, Christ or Gandhi. They have a certain something, we may not know what it is, but we perceive them to be natural leaders. There are not many supervisors/ FLMs who would claim charisma, but they do exist. Charisma is not a very suitable way to appoint a leader for a business organization; this type of person is few and far between, and they do have drawbacks.

Charismatic leaders often fail to realize when it is time for them to go; they are reluctant to train up successors and they may become dogmatic and inflexible in their views. Times and circumstances change but they fail to change with them.

Relying on somebody with charisma to emerge to lead one may be a very hit and miss approach: one cannot advertise for it, but we probably all recognize it when we see it.

The initial power source for a charismatic leader is 'personal power'.

THINK POINT

Think of some other charismatic leaders from the worlds of politics and business. What happened to them? Is there a pattern?

Traditional leaders

One way of choosing leaders in the past (and to some extent in the present day) was to give the leadership role to somebody because it ran in the family. This was (and is) not only a phenomenon of monarchies but of politicians and many businesses. Many a son and daughter has found themselves at the head of a business when they would rather have another career.

The system has both merits and drawbacks. People are brought up in an atmosphere that expects them to assume the leadership role for the country, the party or the business, and thus they are likely to be familiar with the personalities and processes they will meet. Unfortunately, succession to the leadership position may occur whether or not they have any ability at all to fulfil it. This is where the system breaks down. The person may have been trained for the role but that is no guarantee that he or she has the necessary aptitudes. Sometimes it works, especially if they possess a degree of charisma – take for example Churchill, Kennedy or Prince Charles. Often it doesn't: think of George III, or the many sons and daughters who inherited successful organizations only to see them collapse, or the 'from rags to riches to rags in three generations' syndrome. It was this situation that

Weber wished to overcome with his concept of bureaucracy, as discussed in chapter 3.

Giving somebody a leadership role because it runs in the family may be a very unwise move.

Traditional leaders use 'position' power as their major source.

Situational leaders

In his book, *The Admirable Crichton* (1914), J. M. Barrie tells the story of a family shipwrecked on a desert island. Only the butler, Crichton, has any of the skills necessary for survival – he soon became the leader; that is, until they were rescued, when he reverted back to his role of butler.

Crises often throw up somebody who takes charge and sees the organization through the crises and then seems almost to disappear. This is the situational leader, the person who possess the skills and attributes necessary for a particular situation and to whom even more senior staff may defer – for as long as that situation lasts.

Hoping that somebody will emerge who can take the lead when a crisis occurs is a very short-sighted view – leaders are needed in good times as well as bad.

A situational leader will rely on 'expert' or 'resource' power.

Appointed leaders

The usual practice in most countries is to appoint leaders (including supervisors and managers) on the basis of proven ability. Unfortunately this can also lead to what has become known as 'the Peter Principle' – promotion to the level of incompetency. Most supervisory/FLM appointments are made on the basis of a person's ability with the task, and on the basis of opinion, informed and uninformed, about their leadership abilities. The problem is that the only way to see if a person will make a good supervisor, manager or leader is to make them one. If they are competent, all well and good; if they are not, then the problem of what to do with them arises. It is difficult to demote them as this can lead to questions about the competence of those making the appointment. Hence adequate recruitment and selection procedures are important.

Obviously, if leadership ability has been proven in a junior appointment, it is more likely to occur as the person moves up the hierarchy, although sooner or later a position will be reached where the person was better in their last job than their new one. Ability at one level is no guarantee of ability at another.

'Position power' is likely to be a major source for the appointed leader.

A study of the different types of leader is useful, not because it allows for the pigeon-holing of types (very few leaders would fit into one category to the exclusion of all the others), but because it gives a language to talk about leadership which can be used to define the optimum leadership type for the work situation.

What is required in the world of work are leaders who combine the strengths of the above types but minimize the weaknesses. Such a leader will possess knowledge, have a recognized position within the organization and will have been carefully selected. They will not let personal goals and ideas interfere with organizational ones, and they will appreciate the contributions of others. They will be prepared to hand over the leadership role to experts, when necessary, in the interest of task efficiency. They will be secure in their role and be able to delegate to their subordinates. Such a leader is known as a *functional* leader. Their position is secured by what they do rather than who they are. They are able to adapt their leadership role to meet changing situations. They are leaders because they behave like leaders.

It is the supervisor/FLM as a functional leader that is considered in the rest of this chapter. Even if the leader achieves their position by charismatic, traditional, situational or appointed leadership routes, an understanding of functional leadership can assist them in being more effective and perhaps remaining in a leadership position longer.

LEADERSHIP STYLES

A simple way of characterising leadership behaviour is to consider the balance between the leader's concern for people and their concern for the task. Work in the USA during the 1950s showed that groups led by supervisors who were 'people oriented' tended to be more productive than those whose supervisors were 'task oriented'. This work is considered in depth by Robert Blake and Jane Mouton, who produced a grid of leadership styles (figure 9.1).

We shall now look at each of the five categories in figure 9.1 in turn.

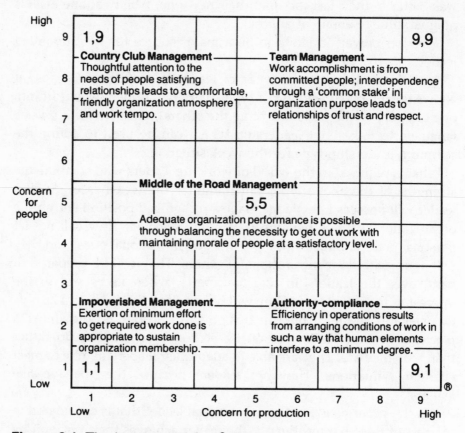

Figure 9.1 The Leadership Grid® Figure
Source: Leadership Dilemmas – Grid® Solutions, by Robert R. Blake and Anne Adams McCanse. Houston: Gulf Publishing Company, p. 29. Copyright © 1991, by Scientific Methods, Inc. Reproduced by permission of the owners.

Impoverished management Little concern about production and little concern about people. Here is a supervisor/manager/leader who has given up. Perhaps they are near retirement, perhaps morale is low, perhaps they have domestic problems; whatever the cause, they are no longer fulfilling a leadership role. Their attitude transmits itself to their subordinates, and not only does the task of the organization suffer but so does the web of relationships within the affected group.

Authority-compliance management The leader who concerns him or herself solely with the production axis is neglecting an important leadership function: the relationships between people. In times of crises it may be necessary to be completely production-centred, but that cannot last long. People need to know that they matter as individuals and that their needs are being considered.

Country club management The opposite of production-centred management. The country club style is very comfortable and relationships are good. People enjoy the social aspects but the jobs are not being given enough emphasis. Country club style puts the group and not the customer first, and in the long term can be as dissatisfying as task management.

Management team A high emphasis on people coupled with a high concern for production was found to produce the best result. The concern for people and an emphasis on quality leads to a team approach to tasks and increased efficiency and productivity. This is the ideal position and the one the supervisor/FLM should aim for.

Middle of the road management The usual state of affairs. The leader at work has an average concern for people and an average concern for production (see figure 9.2).

A truly competent functional leader operates as a (9, 9) leader of a management team, but even if that is beyond some people they can still ensure that they achieve a suitable balance between their concern for people and their concern for production.

Remembering the list of leadership qualities cited earlier, a good leader needs to care about people but must also be able to take hard decisions. If these are seen to be fair they are more likely to be accepted.

Tannenbaum and Schmidt considered that there was a continuum of leadership styles ranging from authoritarian to democratic, depending on the degree of involvement that the manager allowed subordinates in decision-making (figure 9.3).

The supervisor/FLM who adopts a more democratic approach is likely to obtain a more effective use of staff, because they will be more willing to put forward ideas. However, there are times when all supervisors/FLMs will need to make a decision and tell people what it is. Times of crisis may not afford the luxury of group decision-making, but at the end of the crisis the supervisor/FLM should allow time for discussion and involve the group both in the evaluation of how things went and the reasons for the more authoritarian approach.

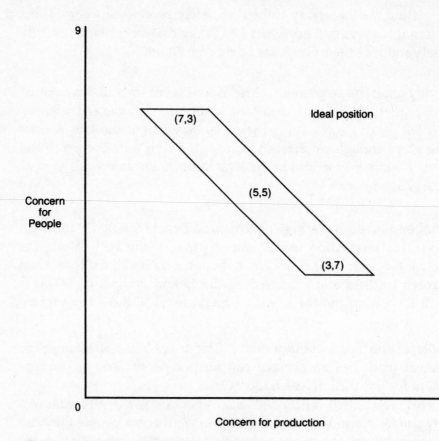

Figure 9.2 The middle of the road leader

John Adair's model of leadership (mentioned in the previous chapter) concentrates on the need to maintain a balance between the:

- needs of the task
- needs of the group
- needs of the individual

You will remember from the previous chapter that it is illustrated as in figure 9.4.

If any of the needs begins to predominate for too long, then the leader has a problem and must redress the balance. For instance, if staff have been involved in long hours solving a problem, the leader should make some time available for meeting group needs, perhaps an afternoon social event. In a similar vein, the leader who tends towards a 'country club' approach which meets group needs at the

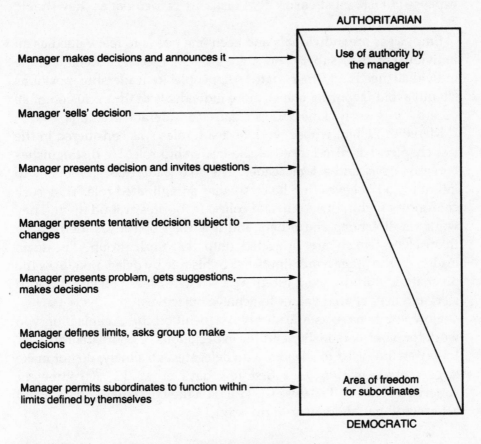

Figure 9.3 A continuum of leadership styles
Reprinted by permission of *Harvard Business Review*. An extract from
Tannenbaum and Schmidt, 1973; copyright © 1973 by the President and
Fellows of Harvard College, all rights reserved.

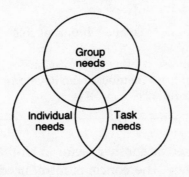

Figure 9.4 The Adair leadership model

expense of task, must ensure that tasks are carried out as they should be.

Employees are individuals and each one needs to feel valued as an individual by their supervisor. A good leader also takes account of the individual needs of their staff. All people in leadership positions should avoid favouring one or more individuals to the exclusion of all others – it is easily done and can cause considerable friction.

Meredith Belbin, whose work on team roles was considered in the last chapter, has also looked at the leadership role. He distinguishes between a *solo* and a *team* leader. The solo leader has a tendency to interfere and believes that he or she has an unlimited role. They seek conformity within the group and collect favourites around them. They work via directions and orders and it is their objectives, derived by themselves, which are projected onto the work group. The team leader, on the other hand, limits her or his role by delegation, uses the diversity within the work group as a strength, seeks talent, develops staff and uses shared values to achieve objectives.

How you behave as a leader will depend on the organization you work for, your personality and the expectations of your subordinates. If they are not used to a leader who delegates, go slowly; do not make large changes within your first few days or weeks. A competent supervisor/FLM will analyse the situation they find themselves in and act accordingly: there is no right way.

SUMMARY

Supervisory Management Standards:

Unit C4   Create effective working relationships
          MANDATORY for VQ Level 3
Unit C15 Create effective working relationships
          OPTIONAL for VQ Level 3

Element C4.1 Gain the trust and support of colleagues and team
               members
         C4.3 Minimise conflict in your team
         C15.1 Help team members who have problems affecting their
               performance

This chapter looked at another factor in Unit 6 of the Management Standards: leadership. The concepts introduced linked the work on motivation (chapter 5) and that on groups and teams (chapter 8).

Power is a resource available to the supervisor/FLM, there being a number of types of power: physical, positional, expert, resource, personal.

There is a relationship between accountability, responsibility and the use of delegation; the supervisor/FLM can delegate responsibility but must retain accountability.

There are different types of leaders and leadership styles, the competent supervisor/FLM adopts a style appropriate to the situation and appreciates the need to balance task, group and individual concerns.

RECOMMENDED FURTHER READING

John Adair, *Effective Leadership* (1983).

Chapter 10

Managing Differences

Case Note 29

Jean had two problems that morning: Pauline was late, yet again, and Peter and Alan weren't speaking to each other, a row over an incident in the pub a couple of nights ago.

'Why can't people get on?', she remarked in general, 'I'm supposed to be a supervisor not a referee!'

Being as near to the day-to-day tasks as they are, supervisors/first line managers (FLMs) are often the first to know about differences at work. A competent and sensitive supervisor is also well placed to defuse such situations, but insensitive handling at the supervisory/ FLM level can often exacerbate a situation and can lead to major organizational effects.

This chapter is about resolving, or at least minimizing, the effect of differences and disagreement, and examines the role of the supervisor/FLM in the types of differences encountered within the workplace:

- Between a group of employees and the organization
- Between a single employee and the organization

- Between a group of workers and a single employee
- Between two employees

Where the difference or disagreement is a result of a complaint brought by the organization against an employee it may end up as a *disciplinary* matter, while a situation where the employee has a complaint against the organization is known as a *grievance*. When a group of employees have the same complaint against the organization it is a *collective grievance*.

Should matters not be resolved at an early stage, they may proceed to be dealt with by the formal disciplinary and grievance procedures that organizations are compelled by law to have in place. This chapter first considers the causes of differences and disagreements, especially the role of change in creating them, then the handling of informal differences and disputes is examined. Finally, the chapter considers the supervisor/FLM's role as a counsellor.

The next chapter considers the legal and procedural aspects to the supervisor/FLM's role as a manager of people.

Differences and disputes can occur from a number of causes. Let us look at the example of persistent lateness, a cause for dispute between Jean and Pauline.

THINK POINT

What reasons may there be for a member of staff being late, not just on the odd occasion but with regularity?

The person may be lazy and unable to get out of bed, but there may also be reasons connected with transport, domestic problems, or medical problems. The latter problems may be better dealt with via counselling rather than disciplining the person. Of course, if they are not resolved, then discipline may be the ultimate course of action.

WHAT CAUSES DIFFERENCES AND DISAGREEMENT?

THINK POINT

Consider any disagreements you have had in the past. What was the root cause behind each one?

There are six main causes of disagreement. Depending on the situation, a potential conflict situation may be created by:

Inaccurate, misleading or incomplete information

The transmission of information between people and people, people and organizations and between organizations is a complex process which is considered in depth in volume 3 of *In Charge* (*Managing Finance and Information*), but the process can be simplified for our study of the management of difference as follows.

There are two parties to the transmission of any piece of information, the *sender* and the *receiver*.

Information exists as thought patterns in the brain. Even when two computers communicate, they are transmitting and receiving information that originated in the brain of the human being who inputted the data used to produce the information.

Thoughts need to be 'coded' into a form suitable for transmission – usually language (see figure 10.1).

It is important that the sender and the receiver use the same, or understand each other's language. Language is not just the national

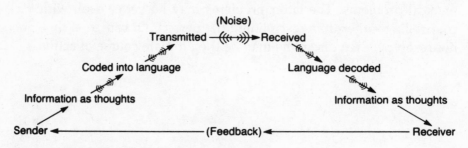

Figure 10.1 Communicating information

language such as English, French or German, it includes the organizational language. Different organizations have their own languages of communication. For example, the acronym APU is used by both the teaching profession and the airline industry. To the former it stands for 'Assessment of Performance Unit', to the latter for 'Auxiliary Power Unit'. To a railway worker EMU represents 'Electrical Multiple Unit', but to a politician it stands for 'European Monetary Union'. It is vital that the parties concerned understand each other's language.

Once the language – verbal, written, computer code etc. – has been agreed, then a message can be transmitted and received. Messages can be interfered with and meanings changed, as in the game of 'Chinese whispers'. This process is known as *noise*. Noise results in the message as sent being perceived as something else after transmission.

The information must then be *decoded* from language to patterns in the brain of the receiver. You will consider this process in more depth in the *Managing Finance and Information* volume of *In Charge*, but suffice to say at this point that what the sender thinks they said or wrote is not always what the receiver perceives the message to be. *Feedback* should be employed to check that the right information has been put over. The Light Brigade were never ordered to charge the Russian Guns; their commanders thought that was what the order said, but its originator meant something quite different and neither party checked back to ensure that they were in agreement.

Inappropriate or incompatible goals

In the '7S Model' (chapter 4), Peters and Waterman saw 'shared values' as being at the centre of any effective management system. Their original term for shared values was *superordinate goals*, goals which override all others within an organization. It should be clear by this stage that individuals and groups can have goals that may be at odds with those of the organization. Do you remember this case note from chapter 5?

Case Note 30

Jean had a problem. Organization reviews tend to lead to a great deal of documentation, and one particular report needed priority treatment. She asked Mike, one of her staff, if he would be prepared to work overtime on Thursday night, when the last pieces of the report would be available, so as to ensure that it would be ready for the Council committee meeting on the Friday.

Jean knew that Mike wanted to buy a new video camera so she thought that the money would be useful.

However, when she approached him she was a little surprised by the answer.

'I have to go to my son's school that night, he's in a concert and it starts at 6.30,' he told her.

'But it is important that we have this report ready and I know you need the money,' replied Jean.

'No,' said Mike; 'It's true that I want the money, but I actually need to watch my son.'

Much of the time there might be little incompatibility between Mike's goals and the organization's, but in the case above they are diametrically opposed. As a supervisor there will be times when the organization requires you to do something that you may disagree with; it is a question of judgement as to how far you will subjugate your goals to superordinate ones. Similarly you need to be aware of your staff's goals and to try to ensure that they have opportunities to achieve them. Compromise, the art of meeting somebody half way, can be a useful skill.

THINK POINT

Have there been times when your goals have conflicted with those of the organization you worked for? How did you resolve the dilemma?

Family holidays offer a good example of conflicting and even incompatible goals.

Case Note 31

Jean and her family were planning two weeks abroad. Her husband wanted a beach to laze on and a quiet hotel; Jean was happy with a quiet hotel but would rather visit places of interest and soak up local atmosphere. Her 17-year-old son wanted lots of night life and plenty of sport. Her 14-year-old daughter wanted to go on holiday with her friends, but they didn't want to go abroad . . .

How do you rationalize these conflicting goals?

There is no right or wrong answer, but it is quite probable that you recognize the scenario and the role that compromise plays.

Task disagreements

We all have our own preferred way of doing things. Many organizations have *standard operating procedures* that lay down how tasks should be carried out. Where these do not exist, you as a supervisor/ FLM may have to decide whether or not a different way of working is acceptable. You need to keep an open mind, but be aware of organizational practices.

If the new idea is one of yours, you need to be tactful in the way you present it to your superior. If it is an idea that has been presented to you, ensure that the person making the suggestion knows that his or her ideas are being taken seriously and that you tell the person why you are not using their idea, if that is the case.

As we will see when examining change, one reason why ideas are not taken on board is because 'we don't do it that way here', or 'we've always done it this way'. These are not very acceptable reasons to give to a person suggesting a change unless they are accompanied by a plausible explanation. Avoid using them.

THINK POINT

Have you felt that you have known a better way of carrying out a task at work?

How did you 'sell' your ideas, who to, and what was the result?

Did your superiors have information that was unavailable to you, and did that information affect their views about your ideas?

Personal feelings

One source of difference, dispute and even outright conflict can be found in personal antagonism. People do not always like their colleagues and there is no way that the organization, or you as a supervisor/FLM, can force people to like each other or be friends. You can insist, however, that personal differences are not allowed to interfere with the task.

Dissatisfaction with working conditions

Working conditions may include the physical environment, pay, holiday entitlements, redundancy conditions etc. Any dissatisfaction with these, especially if it comes from a group of workers, can lead to friction and conflict.

The section of this chapter on grievance covers the role of the supervisor/FLM in such collective disputes, a role that can be difficult and require tact and sensitivity.

Change

Change is very difficult to achieve without upsetting somebody.

The problem with change is that however much we might want it, we can never be sure how it will turn out, and thus we are forced to relate to the situation as it existed before. This situation is often referred to as 'the good old days', whether they were or not.

Kurt Lewin, an American, has developed an interesting way of looking at change which many supervisors have found extremely useful when they are required to implement organizational changes.

Lewin proposes that although change can be planned, the outcome is never certain. Were change incremental (in small, planned steps) or smooth then life would be simple – changes would be small and non-threatening (see figures 10.2 and 10.3). However, the reality is more like figure 10.4.

Change in the real world involves rapid movement from a stable position to a new position, which then stabilizes before the next rapid movement. The reasons for the change are often external and may include product changes, legislation, economic factors etc. The sudden movement from a stable position can be very threatening. The

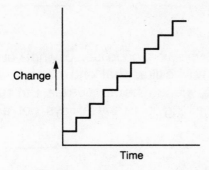
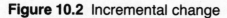
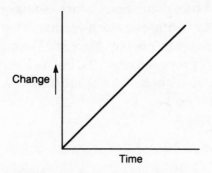

Figure 10.2 Incremental change

Figure 10.3 Smooth change

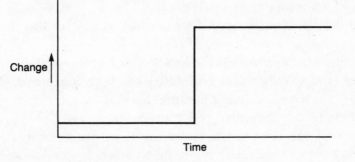

Figure 10.4 Real change

concept is that the stable position must first be broken up into an unstructured amorphous one and that it will then reform into a new position; the difficulty is that it is impossible to predict with accuracy the exact form of the new position.

> **THINK POINT**
>
> Moving house: you may have a very good idea of what your new home and neighbourhood will be like, what kind of people will be living there, how your family will find the facilities etc. But can you be absolutely sure? Something is nearly always not as you thought it would be.

Lou Tice of the Pacific Institute in Seattle has coined the term *comfort zone* (1989) to describe those situations which we have become used to and would rather stay with or return to than change. The negative aspects of change frighten people. Your staff can probably see the positive aspects of any proposed changes, but as a supervisor/ FLM you need to make sure that their worries are addressed if you wish them to take the changes on board.

Case Note 32

Jean had a new idea for the flow of work which she thought would be of benefit to the section and the staff, especially as it would involve them in less tasks each. Mr Rawlings thought that it would work and it should make most tasks easier.

Jean put the changes into a memo and waited for the congratulations.

She was surprised when the local NALGO representative asked to see her, and told her that her staff were very concerned about the changes she intended implementing.

'But everybody benefits,' she argued.

'The staff can see the plus sides but there are a number of things worrying them: will promotion be affected because some people won't have had as much experience in as many tasks? How will rosters be affected? And so on,' was the reply. 'Have these things been considered?'

Jean had thought about all the pluses but had failed to take into account the minuses, and it is the minuses that prevent people leaving their comfort zone. A competent supervisor/FLM will look at all aspects of a change and not push it through based only on the positive aspects. No matter how good the idea is, there will always be people who feel threatened.

Especially when coming into a new job, assess situations before making changes, because your staff will be worried about having a new supervisor. Don't compound it by making changes that are not urgent.

Resistance to change can be alleviated by allowing free discussion where possible, and making sure that everybody involved knows what is going on and why it is happening.

The preceding sections have looked at the reasons for difference within the workplace. The following examines the types of differences and disputes that occur and then provides strategies for dealing with them.

INFORMAL DIFFERENCES AND DISAGREEMENTS

Informal differences and disagreements are those where the use of a formal, organizational procedure to achieve a solution would be inappropriate, at least in the first instance. An example was provided earlier in the chapter: Jean had a problem because Peter and Alan were not speaking to each other as a result of an incident outside work. Whatever happened to cause this rift, it is not Jean's role to solve the initial problem, but she does need to take action to ensure that their feelings for each other do not interfere with their work and the work of others. Members of staff do not need to like each other, nor must they be friends; they must, however, cooperate with each other to achieve the organization's objectives. If personal considerations begin to affect work, then the matter may be formalized and organizational disciplinary procedures implemented.

FORMAL DIFFERENCES AND DISPUTES

These occur when there is some form of conflict between the organization and an individual or group of individuals.

All employees have rights. Before employment begins the only rights are those relating to sexual or racial discrimination during the recruitment and selection process. After appointment there are duties incumbent upon the employer and the employee both through legislation and at Common Law. Common Law is where there is no Act of Parliament, but over a long period of time precedents have become part of the justice system. For example, there is no legislation relating to common assault, but everybody knows that it is against the law.

The duties of employers are:

- Payment of wages for any work done
- Reimbursement of expenses relating to work done (expenses must be reasonable and incurred as a direct result of work)
- To obey the law and not to require an employee to break the law
- To treat employees with respect
- To provide a safe working environment (the Health and Safety at Work Act is covered in depth in volume 2, *Managing Operations*)

The main duties of employees are:

- To obey lawful and reasonable instructions
- To act in a loyal and trustworthy manner
- To take reasonable care within the work situation

Definitions of loyalty and trustworthiness depend on the organizational situation. A member of staff with responsibilities for monies may be treated differently to one without such responsibilities if, say, they were both convicted for shoplifting. In the former case it could be argued that by committing such an offence outside work, the person's trustworthiness within work had been called into question to such a degree that dismissal might be considered.

The Employment Protection (Consolidation) Act 1978, hereafter referred to as the EPA, was passed so as to bring much of the employment legislation and common law into one piece of legislation. Hence the term 'consolidation'.

One aspect of the EPA is that it requires employers to provide a statement of the main terms of an employee's contract of employment within thirteen weeks of the start of employment.

A contract of employment exists from the moment an employee starts a new job. Such a contract is usually, but legally does not have to be, in writing, and forms the basis for conditions of service, pay etc. Whilst the contract need not be in writing, the EPA states that all employees must receive a written statement of their terms and conditions together with details of the organization's disciplinary and grievance procedures. The written statement *must* contain:

- The names of the employer and the employee
- The date employment commenced
- The formal job title
- Pay details
- Hours to be worked
- Holiday arrangements and payments
- Arrangements for sickness
- Period of notice
- Disciplinary procedures
- Grievance procedures
- Pension rights

The EPA applies to the majority of workers in full-time employment. The main exceptions are Crown employees, some overseas based staff and certain merchant seamen and fishermen.

Part-time staff working over 16 hours per week and those who work between 8 and 16 hours per week and have done so for a minimum of 5 years are also covered by the EPA.

Changes to the written statement must be agreed between the employer and the employee.

Other areas of the EPA which may have a direct implication for the relationship between supervisors/FLMs and their staff are:

- The right to reasonable time off for public duties, e.g. jury service, service as a Justice of the Peace, local councillor, member of a tribunal, health authority, school governing body; or as a member of certain sections of the reserve forces. Such time off may well be without pay.
- Time off for trade union duties where the employee is a recognized trade union official. Time off is also a right for the safety representatives of trade unions. Time off for trade union activities, where those activities relate to an official function, is normally paid time off, within reason.

Many disciplinary actions and grievances are a result of disputes relating to terms and conditions of employment. These areas will be explored in more detail in the next chapter.

RESOLVING DIFFERENCES

Issuing a warning or some other form of punishment may not solve the problem in the long term. At the heart of any difference there is usually a personal relationship.

The supervisor/FLM has a restricted number of courses of action for resolving differences, as he or she can only act within organizational guidelines.

Compromise is a skill worth practising. The art of compromise is to aim for a 'win/win' situation rather than a situation in which one side in a dispute is the winner while the other loses, or indeed a situation in which both sides lose. A matter affecting Jean serves to illustrate the point:

Case Note 33

Adrian was thinking of leaving: he believed that Jean was not using his skills to the fullest and that he wasn't being given any responsibility. Jean thought that he was too inexperienced for major responsibilities and, anyway, there were no promotion posts available. Adrian grumbled and Jean found herself picking on him; a classic grievance/disciplinary starting point. Adrian believed, with some justification, that Jean was jealous of his academic qualifications, which were somewhat better than hers. Jean believed that Adrian was after her job.

They sat down after work one evening to discuss the problem between them.

It was a stormy meeting at the beginning, but slowly a compromise began to appear. Adrian could gain the responsibility and experience he required by undertaking a number of special projects under Jean's control. They would both gain from the successful completion of these projects: Adrian would have to move towards Jean and she would have to move from her position towards him, a classic compromise that should benefit the whole organization.

A similar situation is often found during wage negotiations. The employees ask for a 20 per cent rise, the organization offers 2 per cent; if negotiations can be kept going, the settlement will be between 9 per cent and 13 per cent. Each side can claim a degree of victory and nobody feels that they have lost out entirely.

A useful technique to remember whenever there is a conflict situation is the '5R' method:

Recognize that there is a problem and gather as many facts as possible;

Reflect upon the causes of the problem and possible solutions;

Respond, assertively but not aggressively, by stating your perception of the problem to ensure that it is the same as everybody else's, listen to the views of others, and seek clarification and further information if necessary. Let others know your views;

Review the information with those involved and;

Record: if the matter moves to a formal situation, adequate records will be essential.

COUNSELLING

You may recall that Pauline couldn't get up in the morning, but the reasons for her lateness could have been caused by a number of domestic issues.

The solution to any problem, be it work related or domestic, lies in the hands of those involved. You cannot solve people's problems for them.

Wherever the problem lies, if it begins to affect work performance the supervisor/FLM has a major role in ensuring that a solution is arrived at.

Counselling is a process of listening and support that allows people to seek solutions to their own problems, but with help and facilitation from those around them.

Michael Reddy, in his book *The Manager's Guide to Counselling at Work*, defines counselling as: 'A set of techniques, skills and attitudes to help people manage their own problems using their own resources.' Unless a problem is so serious that disciplinary action is the only course (a serious assault on a colleague, dishonesty etc.), the competent supervisor/FLM should attempt to counsel before acting as a policeman or policewoman for the organization.

Counselling involves listening and guiding the employee towards a solution they can own. Imposing your own solution is not usually successful.

Reddy makes the point that his definition speaks of managing a problem and not solving it. Many work and domestic problems, especially those concerned with relationships, do not have complete solutions in the short term; those concerned, including the super-visor/FLM will need to develop strategies to manage and contain the situation to ensure minimum task disruption.

Most supervisors/FLMs receive little training for their counselling role, and yet they are likely to be the first person a member of staff turns to when a problem occurs.

This section of *Managing People* does not seek to provide profes-sional training in counselling, but rather to provide the supervisor/FLM with ideas that they can use when confronted with a request for assistance by one of their staff.

A simple six-step model can be used to explain the role of the supervisor in the counselling process (figure 10.5).

AVAILABILITY
↓
PERCEPTION
↓
UNDERSTANDING
↓
CLARIFYING
↓
RESOURCING
↓
SUPPORTING

Figure 10.5 The six-step counselling model

Availability

Tom Peters, of Peters and Waterman '7S' fame, has coined the phrase 'management by wandering about' (MBWA) to describe a pheno-menon prevalent in successful organizations. Supervisors and managers should be in contact with their subordinates and not cossetted in offices. As the first point of contact for any problems, the supervisor needs to be available for informal contact. A trip to the supervisor's office may be viewed as intimidating by some em-ployees, and as containing elements of formality. That can come later; initial contact is best made in a place where the employee feels com-fortable, on their territory. It may only be a request to speak with the supervisor/FLM privately, but at least an initial move has been made. This can only occur if the supervisor is *available*. MBWA also allows the supervisor to gather information about what is happening within his or her section of the organization and to exercise the next stage of the six-step model: their perception.

Perception

Case Note 34

Jean was on one of her walkabouts. She used them to chat to the staff, being careful not to interrupt their work too much.

Paul was preparing the graphs for a report on the desk-top publishing system. Paul was well liked and his normal practice was to hum snippets from the most popular TV adverts as he worked. Today he was silent.

'Everything okay Paul?' asked Jean.

'Yes, not so bad,' came the rather blunt reply.

Jean walked on and then stopped. This wasn't like Paul. She turned and looked at him. His countenance was not the cheery one everybody had come to expect. He looked downright miserable.

She asked one of his friends whether everything was all right.

'He's been very quiet this morning, but those graphics are very complicated.'

Jean left the DTP suite and continued her walk round. 'I'll go back later,' she thought, 'something's not right there.'

In chapter 3, the 11 competences developed by Burgoyne and Stuart were examined. One of these was 'continuing sensitivity to events'. The supervisor/FLM who is visible in the workplace and makes time to talk to subordinates is likely to find that they become more perceptive to the way those subordinates are feeling and can tell when something is wrong.

Case Note 35

Jean was right, something was wrong. A telephone call summoned her back to the DTP suite. Paul's screen was blank, papers were all over the floor and Paul was nowhere to be seen.

'He just flipped,' said one of his colleagues. 'One minute we were all working normally and the next he'd thrown the report all over the office, yanked the plug from the machine, said what he thought about working here and stormed out.'

'Where is he now?' asked Jean.

'Roger from over the corridor caught up with him and took him down to the canteen. Paul was really upset about something and we've no idea what.'

Because she made a point of getting to know and talking to her staff on a regular basis, Jean had already guessed that something was wrong. Her next task was to find out exactly what it was and what she could do about it.

Understanding

Having identified that there is a problem, the competent supervisor/ FLM needs to come to an understanding of what the problem is and how it has arisen. Only with that information to hand can the subordinate receive effective support.

Case Note 36

By the time Jean reached the canteen, Paul had calmed down. Roger took her to one side as she came in.

'I thought I'd better have a word,' he said, 'I haven't been able to find out much, but I know Paul has been putting in long hours and there's something wrong at home. Perhaps he'll open up more to you.'

Jean sat down with Paul and said very little. She'd always believed in the old adage that the less you say, the more you'll hear.

Gradually the story came out: Paul's eldest daughter, who was eight, was in trouble at school; her work had deteriorated and she'd been in trouble for her behaviour in the playground. Paul's wife was at home during the day with their two-year-old twins, and a furious row had broken out when Paul had been told about the problems at school. His wife blamed him because he was leaving home early and didn't seem to have enough time for his children. He couldn't understand her comments; after all, he was trying to make sure they could pay all their bills. Last night his wife had taken the children and was now staying with a friend. Paul was distraught and couldn't understand what was happening.

Clarifying

Once a problem is out in the open, the task of finding the underlying cause can begin. In the case above, the problem is a domestic issue between Paul and his wife seemingly caused by Paul's work pattern, but what is the underlying cause?

THINK POINT

What do you believe is the underlying cause of the problem Paul is encountering? There may be a number of issues, and you have very little information, but use your knowledge of the people *you* work with to make a list of possible prime causes.

It is clear that Paul's problems stem from his work pattern, but why is he working such long hours – does he need overtime? does he prefer being at work to being at home? has he an unreasonable workload? is he having problems with the tasks he has been given?

The first two reasons are probably beyond Jean's control, although she could help arrange financial or marriage guidance counselling if Paul and his wife were agreeable. The latter two causes are within her control: she can examine workloads and provide training if necessary.

To find the fundamental cause of a problem, the supervisor/FLM needs to look at the factors behind the difficulties and then consider whether there are actions they can take to assist the subordinate (or colleague) directly, or whether they should advise the seeking of help from other quarters.

Case Note 37

Jean and Paul went back to her office. The problem seemed to be that everybody wanted to use Paul's creativity and expertise in desktop publishing. Paul, with a young family, found the money useful and accepted more work than he could reasonably handle. His easygoing nature made it difficult for him to refuse requests for his services. This put further pressure on him until he cracked. The last straw was a minor thing; he'd accidentally deleted two pages of work on the machine and that was enough to 'make him blow his top'.

The underlying cause was Paul's need for extra cash coupled with his wish not to say no to requests. Jean had been happy to see that people wanted to use the service her section offered and thought that the quality was so high, but she hadn't thought of the pressure that this was putting on Paul. After all, he seemed happy with the situation.

Resourcing

People solve their own problems, others can only assist. It is important that if a person has a problem that they 'own' the solution. In the case of Paul, he has to decide how much he wants to work and how much time he should dedicate to his family. The supervisor/FLM (in this case Jean) has a role in providing the necessary resources to enable the employee to implement a solution.

Case Note 38

Jean and Paul looked at the DTP work schedules.

'I want to do the work for people, they've come to rely on me,' said Paul, 'and some extra money does come in handy.'

'What other work have you at the moment?' asked Jean.

'I'm involved in this training programme for new staff that's taking up a great deal of time, and that's another evening that I don't get home until late.'

Jean thought about it: if she could use one of the people Paul was training, she could take the pressure off him and ensure that all the work was completed in time. There would still be enough extra work for Paul to obtain some overtime and she would request an upgrading for him at the next review. She didn't expect that any of the senior managers on the review panel would object – they were all making use of Paul's services.

Paul agreed that this would help and the opportunity to work alongside somebody he had trained would be a useful experience.

Supporting

Problems are rarely solved overnight. The final stage of the six-step model involves the supervisor/FLM monitoring the situation and providing on-going support.

THE ASSERTIVE SUPERVISOR/FRONT LINE MANAGER

The style of the competent supervisor should be assertive, especially when dealing with differences and problems. Assertiveness is not the same as aggression. Aggression occurs when a person puts their wants and needs above those of others. An aggressive person gets their own way by allowing others no choice at all; they will bully or threaten until they get their own way.

A person who is non-assertive or non-aggressive is unlikely to be in a supervisory/FLM position because they are very compliant. If they are promoted into such a position they will be very unhappy. Being unassertive is, in a way, the opposite of aggression rather than the opposite of assertion in that a non-assertive person will generally put the needs and wants of others above their own. A non-assertive person may be inclined to back down even when they are right, and this can have dire consequences.

An assertive person has the balance right. The assertive person respects the needs and wants of others and sees them as equal to his or her own. Assertiveness is about being honest, frank, forthright but not domineering; it is active rather than passive. To be assertive rather than aggressive the supervisor/FLM needs to negotiate rather than insist, influence rather than bully and listen at least as much as they talk.

SUMMARY

Supervisory Management Standards:

Unit C4   Create effective working relationships
           MANDATORY for VQ Level 3

Unit C15   Create effective working relationships
           OPTIONAL for VQ Level 3

Element   C4.1   Gain the trust and support of colleagues and team
                members
           C4.3   Minimise conflict in your team
           C15.1 Help team members who have problems affecting their
                performance

Differences at work can occur for a number of reasons and the supervisor/FLM is likely to be one of the first to have to deal with the problems they cause.

Faulty communications are often a cause of differences and disputes, and the competent supervisor needs to ensure that lines of communication are clear and that feedback is employed to ensure understanding.

Change can be very disturbing and is often a source of conflict; people do not like to be moved too far away from their 'comfort zone'.

Terms and Conditions of Employment are covered by the Employment Protection (Consolidation) Act.

The competent supervisor is prepared to listen to their staff and to act in a counselling role, assisting and supporting but allowing individuals to own their own problems.

RECOMMENDED FURTHER READING

Sam R. Lloyd, *How to Develop Assertiveness* (1988).
Michael Reddy, *The Manager's Guide to Counselling at Work* (1987).

Chapter 11

Managing Discipline, Grievance, Discrimination and Dismissal

Supervisory Management Standards:

Unit C15 Create effective working relationships
           OPTIONAL for VQ Level 3

Element C15.1 Help team members who have problems
                  affecting their performance
           C15.2 Contribute to implementing disciplinary and
                  grievance procedures

DISCIPLINE

Case Note 39

'Did you take money out of the Christmas Club?' Jean asked Diane. The tears told the answer.

The disciplinary procedure for Jean's employer clearly stated that theft was an offence for which summary dismissal was a suitable sanction.

'Am I going to be sacked?' Diane whispered, 'I've got three children to look after; I have taken a few pounds but I've always put it back. I was going to the bank this lunchtime. If you hadn't looked at the book and asked about the pencilled-in entries nobody would have known'.

Slowly the story came out. Diane's husband had been made

redundant recently and she was having trouble making ends meet. The sum involved was small and it appeared that although she had been borrowing from the funds, the money had always been returned.

'I'm sorry,' said Jean, 'but I'm going to have to recommend that you're suspended until I can examine the books thoroughly. You've had a copy of the disciplinary procedure and I think that you need to talk to somebody from your union. I'm sorry to sound so formal, but this is a serious matter and I intend to follow the procedures to the letter. I've got to inform Mr Rawlings. Perhaps you'd like to wait outside until I can tell you exactly what is happening.'

THINK POINT

Rules are rules: if Jean recommends dismissal, Diane will be dismissed. Even if Jean recommends some other form of sanction she may be overruled.

How would you approach this situation?

How Diane should be dealt with depends on the nature of her job and the circumstances of the case. As a supervisor/FLM you cannot ignore the fact that theft has occurred, however much you like Diane as a person.

A supervisor is unlikely to be making the final decisions on matters which have led to formal disciplinary action, but in such cases, as the front line member of management, the supervisor/FLM will have a key role in providing information and possibly evidence for the proceedings.

The previous chapter looked at ways of resolving differences. Where there is a question of misconduct it is important that there are clearly defined procedures that can be followed. Clearly defined procedures protect both sides in a disciplinary matter; they ensure that all employees are treated equally, and provide the organization with a structure for sanctions on the occasions when they are necessary.

The actual procedures will vary from organization to organization, and you should obtain a copy of your organization's 'disciplinary procedures' and read them in conjunction with this chapter. As stated in the last chapter, you should have received a copy of the procedures as part of your *terms and conditions.*

THINK POINT

How aware are you of your organization's discipline and grievance procedures and your role within them?

Disciplinary action occurs when the organization is in dispute with an individual. Such a dispute may be as a result of the employee not fulfilling their obligations to the employer or committing an act that the employer considers inappropriate for a member of the organization.

This section is not designed to make you an expert in handling such actions from start to finish, but rather to ensure that you understand the procedures that operate within your organization, and that you fulfil your obligations to both the organization and the individual fairly. The supervisor/FLM's role regarding Health and Safety at Work (HASAW) and Care of Substances Hazardous to Health (COSHH) legislation is covered in the *Managing Operations* volume of this series, while payment systems, tax and National Insurance are included in *Managing Finance and Information*.

Case Note 40

Pauline's lateness was beginning to affect the work schedules and was causing resentment among the staff.

'If she can be late every other morning, why can't we?' Jean overheard one morning.

'I've got to do something about this,' she thought, and arranged to see Ayesha in the personnel department later that day.

'I've had several quiet words with her and there don't seem to be any problems at home. She says she has trouble getting up and then laughs about it.'

'You need to take some kind of formal action to warn her that this type of behaviour is not appropriate,' Ayesha advised: 'Let's look at the disciplinary procedures and see what would be a reasonable course of action.'

THINK POINT

Using your own organization's procedures as a guide, what would be an appropriate course of action for dealing with Pauline, given that she has had several verbal mentions about her behaviour? How would they have dealt with Diane's case?

Different types of misconduct carry different types of sanctions depending upon the seriousness. In general terms, procedures divide misconduct up into:

- minor infringements
- serious infringements
- gross misconduct

The first times Pauline was late would count as minor infringements; persistent lateness might well be considered as serious infringements; offences such as theft, harassment, assault are likely to be thought of as examples of serious misconduct. An organization's procedures will state the seriousness of different degrees of misconduct and the types of sanction available to management.

The ultimate sanction, usually reserved for the most serious cases of gross misconduct, is summary dismissal. Such a sanction is unlikely to be one that the supervisor/FLM can apply.

The majority of disciplinary procedures follow a similar format:

- *Informal verbal warning* – usually given by the immediate supervisor/FLM; such a warning is 'unofficial' to the extent that no formal record is made. The problem for the supervisor/FLM is that it is difficult to judge when it is necessary to move to a formal procedure. In the case of Pauline's lateness, how many times must it happen before Jean starts making records and considers taking official action?
- *Verbal warning* following a disciplinary hearing; this type of warning will be recorded on the employee's file for a specified period of time.

- *Written warning*: if the misconduct that led to a verbal warning is repeated or if the offence is considered to be sufficiently serious, a disciplinary hearing can issue a written warning, which is normally considered to be more serious than a verbal one. As with all formal warnings, the employee should be informed what it is they must do to improve the situation or solve the problem, and when the warning will be reviewed.

Your organization's procedure will give details of the types and levels of warnings together with an indication of the levels of management involved.

Whatever the organizational procedures, it is important that the supervisor is aware of the basic principles of a fair disciplinary action.

Failure to follow the correct procedures may result in a claim to an industrial tribunal for unfair dismissal, and this can involve the organization in considerable expense and bad publicity.

A disciplinary procedure should ensure that an employee receives adequate notice of any hearing to be held, and is informed as to rights of representation. After any hearing there should be a clear appeals procedure.

The initiation of a disciplinary action may well be by the supervisor/FLM. Before taking such action you should consider whether you have exhausted all the informal means of resolving the difference. If you have, ensure that you follow the procedures laid down to the letter. If you don't, you will be open to an accusation of unfair or unreasonable behaviour. Upon promotion to a supervisory position ensure that you know how much authority you have and be prepared to seek advice from your line manager or your personnel department if a problem arises.

Whenever a dispute or difference looks like it might lead to formal action, you need to make sure that adequate records of incidents, comments and reactions are kept; they will be needed to support your points and will need to be made available at any hearing.

You may form part of the panel for a disciplinary hearing, but it is equally likely that you will be a witness for one of the two sides. A hearing can only consider matters that the employee has been advised of in advance.

Case Note 41

It was all going wrong!

Pauline had been informed that her timekeeping had become unacceptable. She had, in accordance with the Authority's disciplinary procedures, been informed that a hearing would be held to consider her timekeeping. She was given seven days notice of the hearing and further informed that she could bring a representative or friend with her.

The hearing was underway and Jean was having problems.

She'd kept notes of the three times in the past two weeks that she'd had to speak to Pauline about timekeeping but then she added, 'It's not only her timekeeping but the standard of her work isn't up to scratch any more.'

A very unwise comment.

Whatever the provocation, only matters of which the employee has been informed may be brought up in a disciplinary hearing. The raising of any other matters is deemed to be unreasonable and, if allowed, gives weight to any appeal.

In the case above, Pauline could not be disciplined following Jean's comments. If Jean had a complaint about Pauline's work, sufficient to warrant disciplinary action, Pauline should have been advised that this was also a matter for consideration.

Your organization's procedure will advise you of the sanctions available to hearings. These will range from formal warnings to dismissal. In some organizations they may include fines or demotions. Where a warning has been given, it should contain information as to the offence, what the person can do to rectify the situation, what support they will be given, and how long the warning will stand before it is reviewed and expunged if there has been no recurrence of the offence or an improvement in performance.

Case Note 42

'It's very difficult,' said Mr Rawlings, as the panel considered Diane's case. 'She admits that she, to use her term, borrowed money from the Christmas Club, but she always returned it.'

'Nevertheless, legally that is theft; we could hand the matter over to the police,' the representative of the legal department advised them.

'There's no doubt that it is a dismissal matter, she can't argue with that. Jean, what do the rest of the staff think about her behaviour?' asked Mr Rawlings.

'They're quite sympathetic; after all, the money was returned. I don't believe that she intended to steal from her work mates.'

Diane and her union representative had not denied that she had broken the rules; they had asked for the panel to take account of the problems Diane and her family had been having, and of the fact that Diane had an excellent work record prior to the offence being considered.

Nobody denied that the panel could recommend instant dismissal. However, the procedures of the Authority allowed for lesser punishments if the panel deemed that dismissal might be too harsh a punishment given any mitigating factors.

Diane was offered a position in another section, with a drop in grade (and thus salary) and a final written warning to last for two years. Any repeat of a similar offence would mean instant dismissal. The alternative was her resignation.

Had Diane been in a job where handling cash was a major part of the task, the transfer and demotion option would be unlikely to be offered and she would have been dismissed. As it is, it would be unlikely that Diane would ever be trusted with money again.

Diane agreed to the transfer, but in her heart she knew that she would have to seek another job because the stigma of the theft was likely to stick. At least under present circumstances she would be able to work off the offence and apply to other organizations after her warning was expunged.

EXPUNGING A WARNING

If the performance or attitude of the employee improves and there are no further problems, a warning may be removed (the normal term is expunged) from the employee's record. It should not be referred to again as the problem has been solved. If, however, there is no improvement or the problem keeps occurring, then the supervisor/ FLM will need to consider moving to the next stage of the disciplinary procedures.

Disciplinary action should be about improving performance and remedying problems rather than punishment in all but the most serious of cases.

As a supervisor you will need to decide whether something is a matter for discipline or whether counselling and welfare advice might be a more reasonable course.

GRIEVANCE

Grievance procedures are brought by employees against the organization. Grievance procedures have their set timetables of events and arrangements for hearings and appeals.

It is not unusual to find that the supervisor's/FLM's actions are those which have caused the grievance. This is not necessarily a reason for dismay. If you have been carrying out your duties within the procedures laid down by your organization then there is nothing to fear; if you have exceeded your authority or have acted outside organizational policies then those actions may be the cause of a grievance procedure.

Most formal grievance procedures require the employee to take up the problem with their supervisor in the first instance. If somebody brings such a matter to you, even if it involves you or you think that it is unreasonable, you must still take it seriously and ensure that the employee feels valued.

Many individual grievances can be settled at supervisor level, but those that cannot must be referred to middle/senior management as required by the organization's procedure.

Collective grievances are those brought by a number of staff, all with the same grievance. They may well be represented by a trade union, and as a supervisor/FLM you may well be one of those with a grievance. If this is the case, it is wise to act in such a way as to avoid making enemies after the grievance has been settled. Be careful about what you say; let your personnel department or senior management and the official representatives act; there are special procedures for such collective grievances which will probably involve senior management and employee representatives such as trade unions.

FAIRNESS TO THE EMPLOYEE

The root cause of many individual grievances lies in a belief by an employee that they have been treated unfairly. Some of the rights of employees were covered in the last chapter in the section dealing with the Employment Protection (Consolidation) Act.

All employees have a right not to be discriminated against. There are a number of pieces of anti-discriminatory legislation that the supervisor/FLM needs to be aware of:

Equal Pay Act (1970)

This Act, subsequently amended by the Sex Discrimination Acts of 1975 and 1986, plus European legislation, is concerned with ensuring that men and women receive equal pay for equal or similar work. The Acts appreciate that the work done by men and women might be different and apply the concept of work of equal value.

Sex Discrimination Act 1975

It is unlawful for employers to discriminate against employees on the grounds of gender or marriage. Such discrimination can be direct, i.e., where it is obvious that one sex is treated better than another, or indirect, where it appears that the organization is treating both sexes equally but where reality is different (for instance, the advertisement for the job mentioned nothing about gender but only men were interviewed). For a minority of jobs, gender can be considered a 'genuine occupational qualification' (GOQ): e.g., acting, lavatory attendant etc.

Race Relations Act 1976

Similar to the Sex Discrimination Act, but applies to race and religious affiliations rather than gender. There are a number of exemptions (GOQs): e.g., Indian waiters in Indian restaurants etc.

Maternity Provision

The Employment Protection (Consolidation) Act 1978 (EPA) (see chapter 10), makes provision that entitles pregnant women to:

- Time off for antenatal care
- Maternity pay
- The right to return to work after the birth but not necessarily to the same job
- The right not to be dismissed unfairly
- The right to redundancy pay where appropriate

These rights may well depend on the length of service the employee has with the organization. The amount of time off for antenatal care is not open-ended but should be 'reasonable'.

Should the return to work be impractical, due perhaps to changes in the business, redundancy pay entitlement is available to the employee. This right applies between the eleventh week of pregnancy and the twenty-ninth week after confinement.

Harassment

Staff who feel that they have been harassed for any reason, the usual ones being sexual or racial, are entitled to use the grievance procedures. Many organizations make harassment a disciplinary offence.

Where an employee suspects discrimination, they are entitled to take legal action for damages against the organization.

DISMISSAL

It is unlikely that an individual supervisor/FLM will have the authority to dismiss somebody themselves, however serious the offence; this is usually a function reserved for more senior management. Beware, however, of forcing a member of staff into a resigning position. If you make it unpleasant or so difficult for a member of staff that they feel they must leave, you may have laid your organization open to a charge of *constructive dismissal*, one of the forms of *unfair dismissal*.

Should an employee claim that they have been dismissed unfairly they can take the matter to an industrial tribunal, which may award damages or even reinstatement.

The advice for any supervisor is that you should ensure that you keep adequate records and take no action that may affect disciplinary matters without seeking advice.

According to the EPA and the subsequent 1980 Employment Act, a person has been dismissed fairly if the reasons for that dismissal are related to:

- The employee's conduct (disciplinary procedures must have been followed);
- A statutory duty or restriction which prevents employment continuing: an employee may be dismissed where keeping

them on involves breaking the law. For example, a driver who loses their licence, even if this is outside work, cannot continue working as a driver;

- The employee's capability or qualifications: capability can be related to skills or, indeed, health;
- Redundancy (see below).

Obviously there may be other reasons why an organization may wish to dismiss an employee but the organization will need to show that it has acted in a reasonable manner.

UNFAIR DISMISSAL

Employees who are dismissed may claim that the organization was acting unfairly. The Conditions and Terms of Service will have included the disciplinary procedures (as considered earlier). If Pauline had been dismissed the first time she was late, she might well decide to take the organization to an industrial tribunal (IT) and claim that she had been treated unreasonably, a case she would probably win!

Employees who are dismissed solely because they either join or refuse to join a trade union will be deemed to have been dismissed unfairly; these reasons are known as *inadmissible reasons.*

Not all employees can make representations to an industrial tribunal. Part-time employees who work between 8 and 16 hours per week must have worked for the organization for at least five years; full-time staff must have been employed by the organization for at least two years. These limits do not apply to the inadmissible reasons quoted above.

Where an organization has been merged or taken over, or where there is recognized continuance of employment (e.g., teachers moving from one Local Education Authority to another have continual service), employees are still protected.

Industrial tribunals will seek to establish the reasonableness of an employer's actions: for instance, where an employee could no longer carry out a task because of health reasons and was dismissed, what steps were taken to find alternatives within the organization. If no steps were taken, the dismissal might be found to be unfair; where alternatives were examined but were not suitable from either the individual's or the organization's point of view, the dismissal may be deemed fair.

If an IT finds that a dismissal was unfair or wrongful it can award damages, reinstatement in the same job or re-engagement to a different job.

THINK POINT

As a supervisor/FLM what problems do you foresee if an IT ordered the reinstatement of an employee whose dismissal you had recommended?

A good motto for disciplinary and dismissal matters is that 'you do it right the first time or you don't do it'. If dismissal is found to be unfair, this can cost the organization a great deal both in terms of cash and relationships. Study and follow your organization's procedures and seek advice earlier rather than later.

REDUNDANCY

Every organization goes through ups and downs and there are times when the number of employees need to be reduced. Various organization terms are used to describe this process: restructuring, downsizing, rightsizing etc. Whatever the term, the effect on the staff is likely to be a number of redundancies.

Concern, despair and anger are common reactions to redundancy, affecting as it does the basic needs for security (see the Maslow Model of Motivation discussed in chapter 5), and these feelings are likely to be vented at the supervisor.

There is always the danger that the supervisor/FLM might also be facing a redundancy situation and may therefore be concerned about his or her own security, as well as that of his or her employees.

Redundancies can occur when:

- An organization ceases trading
- An organization is taken over and the pattern of business altered
- An organization changes location
- The demand for work decreases

- New technology is introduced
- Working practices are changed

In cases of redundancy, employees are protected by law. Employers must consult with interested parties, unions or employee representatives. If the organization ceases trading, special provisions are in place to ensure that redundancy payments are received by eligible employees.

Where the work has diminished, the employer needs to show that the criteria for selecting people for redundancy were fair. If the firm has relocated, employees cannot be forced to move home and will be entitled to redundancy payments if they do not wish to move. Redundancy payments do not normally apply to changes in shifts and working hours: allowance for changes such as these are normally written into the contract of employment.

Some employees may opt for redundancy – such a course of action is known as voluntary redundancy. If this occurs, much disruption can be avoided. Pressure should never be brought on an employee to volunteer for redundancy; this would constitute harassment and unfair dismissal.

Hopefully, as a supervisor/FLM, you will deal with relatively few disciplinary or dismissal cases; if you do become involved, remember to keep clear records and follow your organization's procedures to the letter.

SUMMARY

Supervisory Management Standards:

Unit C15 Create effective working relationships
OPTIONAL for VQ Level 3

Element C15.1 Help team members who have problems affecting their performance
C15.2 Contribute to implementing disciplinary and grievance procedures

In any organization, there will be times when formal disciplinary action must be followed as a result of problems that occur.

Terms and Conditions of Employment must contain the procedures to be followed in cases of disciplinary action or where there is a grievance situation.

The role of the supervisor/FLM in disciplinary actions is important as they may well be the initiators of such action.

Failure to follow the correct procedures can lead to charges of unfair dismissal.

Employees are protected from discrimination by law.

RECOMMENDED FURTHER READING

G. A. Cole, *Personnel Management, Theory and Practice* (1988), chapters 35–6.

Chapter 12

Personal Competence

Personal competences are similar whether one is a supervisor/first line manager (FLM), a middle manager or a senior manager. The difference in how they are applied is one of dimension; all those in supervisory and management positions need to consider how they can develop the personal competences within the job and cultural situation they find at work. A consideration of the personal competences shows that they also have a role to play in relation to social and domestic behaviour.

The personal competences most closely allied to the key role area of *Managing People* are firstly those connected with the *management of others*, and secondly with the *management of yourself* (see sections 2 and 3 in figure 12.1).

The personal competences in sections 1 and 4 of figure 12.1 are covered in the *Managing Operations* and *Managing Finance and Information* volumes of *In Charge* respectively.

In Charge approaches the personal competences in the form of an *action plan*. When considering personal competences you should ask yourself:

- How well do I handle this area of personal competence?
- How could I handle it better?
- How does it relate to my functional competence at work?

2 MANAGING OTHERS TO OPTIMIZE RESULTS

Supervising and management is about getting things done through other people. The previous chapters have examined the functional competences needed to achieve the goals of the organization. Personal competences are about the qualities you need to develop to achieve the best results possible, and to this end you need to consider

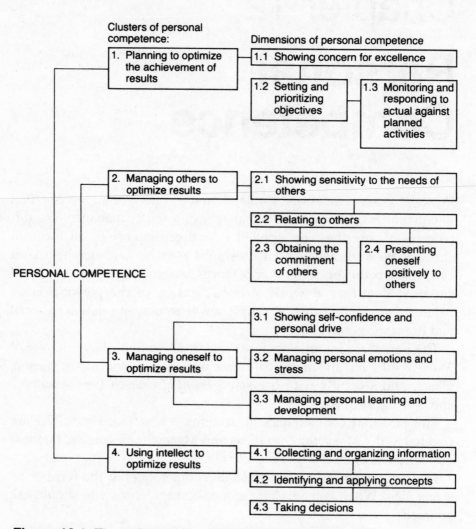

Clusters of personal competence:

Dimensions of personal competence

PERSONAL COMPETENCE

1. Planning to optimize the achievement of results

1.1 Showing concern for excellence

1.2 Setting and prioritizing objectives

1.3 Monitoring and responding to actual against planned activities

2. Managing others to optimize results

2.1 Showing sensitivity to the needs of others

2.2 Relating to others

2.3 Obtaining the commitment of others

2.4 Presenting oneself positively to others

3.1 Showing self-confidence and personal drive

3. Managing oneself to optimize results

3.2 Managing personal emotions and stress

3.3 Managing personal learning and development

4. Using intellect to optimize results

4.1 Collecting and organizing information

4.2 Identifying and applying concepts

4.3 Taking decisions

Figure 12.1 The MCI Personal Competence Model
Permission from MCI.

your relationship with others and the way you manage yourself. There are four areas of personal competence to consider in your relationship with others, as above:

2.1 Showing sensitivity to the needs of others

Sensitivity in a supervisory/managerial sense is the ability to understand how others are thinking. The competent supervisor/FLM develops antennae that allow him or her to understand what is going on and to realize when things are going wrong before they do. Competent supervisors know the people around them and can sense when things are not as they should be. They are receptive to changes in behaviour and look beyond them to the underlying cause.

Sensitive behaviour means not jumping to conclusions, but carefully considering the evidence and signs and then taking the feelings of others into consideration before acting.

THINK POINT

- How sensitive do you believe you are to the feelings and needs of others?
- Can you think of any occasions when you have not responded in a sensitive way? Why was that, and what factors affected your behaviour?
- How would you handle things if a similar situation occurs again?

Consider the following questions:

- Are you satisfied that your response demonstrates your personal competence?
- Do you make time available to support others?
- How do you make others feel that they are doing a good job and how do you reinforce their feelings of esteem?
- Are you patient and understanding with the mistakes and difficulties of others?
- Can you accept that others may hold a different view from your own? Can you understand their viewpoint even if you disagree with it?
- Do you encourage others to express themselves honestly?

Action Plan
What steps can you take to ensure that you show 'sensitivity to the needs of others'?

2.2 Relating to others

Supervisors and managers do not work in isolation. It is not enough to know about motivational theories and interpersonal skills. The competent supervisor/FLM needs to consider how they relate to those around them, be they superiors, colleagues or subordinates, and how their behaviour affects the way those around them relate to each other.

THINK POINT

Are there areas either within or outside of the work situation where you believe you could improve the relationship you have with others?

Consider the following questions:

- Are you satisfied that your response demonstrates your personal competence?
- Do you give honest and constructive feedback?
- Do you state your own opinions clearly?
- Do you encourage discussion of conflicting views to resolve issues?
- Do you try to build working relationships with others, in your department, in the organization, in other organizations?
- Do you develop and use the strengths and skills of others to achieve set objectives?
- Do you encourage others to make the best use of their abilities?
- Can you keep your team/work group focused on the set objectives?

Action Plan
What steps can you take to ensure that you are competent at 'relating to others'?

2.3 Obtaining the commitment of others

However well skilled and trained you are, as a supervisor/FLM you need the commitment of others in order to achieve the objectives your organization has set. Commitment has to be earned; its components are job satisfaction, respect, trust and understanding. Involving your staff in decision-making is likely to aid their commitment as they will have a clearer understanding of 'why' as well as the 'what' and the 'how'. If you have not achieved the commitment of your staff you will have problems raising standards, service etc. above the merely adequate.

THINK POINT

Consider supervisors/FLMs you have worked for: how did they obtain your commitment, are there lessons for you in the way they acted?

Consider the following questions:

- Are you satisfied that your response demonstrates your personal competence?
- Do you explain what is needed to your staff clearly?
- Do your staff understand what is expected of them?
- Can you identify and resolve resistance from your staff?
- Do you explain 'why' something is needed and then relate it to the objectives set for the person/people involved?
- Do you involve your staff in decision-making?

Action Plan
What steps can you take to ensure that you 'obtain the commitment of others'?

2.4 Presenting oneself positively to others

As a supervisor/line manager you hold a leadership position and others will expect you to act as a leader. How you dress, how you act, how you speak etc. will all be indicative of the image you present. The more confident you feel about yourself (to be considered in the next section of personal competences), the more positive an image you will present. As a supervisor/FLM you are moving into a different area of the 'organizational focus' (chapter 5), and you will be representing not just yourself but your section and perhaps the whole organization: dress, speech, manners etc., especially when you are making presentations, leading or taking part in meetings, or even when you are on the telephone, are important if you are to be competent in your expanded role.

THINK POINT

In what ways can you improve your image so as to present yourself more positively?

Consider the following questions:

- Are you satisfied that your response demonstrates your personal competence?
- Can you present ideas and concepts to others in a variety of situations, e.g. in meetings and training sessions, on the telephone, in letters/memos/reports and when communicating one to one?
- Are you aware of the skills needed for successful presentations (covered in *In Charge* volume 3, *Managing Finance and Information*)?
- Can you handle questions and difficult situations in a calm manner?

Action Plan
What steps can you take to ensure that you 'present yourself positively to others'?

Having considered the personal competences relating to the management of others, we now consider those that relate to the management of self.

3 MANAGING ONESELF TO OPTIMIZE RESULTS

3.1 Showing self-confidence and personal drive

The last section mentioned the need for self-confidence if the supervisor/FLM is to present a positive image.

If you wish others to be committed, you need to show commitment yourself; if you want respect you must show respect to others and show respect to yourself. Personal drive comes from an understanding of your job and the skills, the attributes and competence you need, and a knowledge of your personal 'comfort zones' (chapter 10). You cannot expect others to display drive and react positively to change if you cannot do it yourself.

THINK POINT

- How confident do you feel in your own abilities at work?
- How comfortable are you with your supervisory/FLM role?

Consider the following questions:

- Are you satisfied that your response demonstrates your personal competence?
- Are you enthusiastic about the plans and objectives of your organization?
- If you are unhappy about any plans etc. in your organization, do you, wittingly or unwittingly, transmit your feelings to your staff?
- Can you face problems without losing your commitment and drive?
- Can you identify new opportunities and take the initiative to move forward?
- Do you take personal responsibility for making things happen?
- Can you guide and control situations and events?

Action Plan
What steps can you take to ensure that you show 'self-confidence and personal drive'?

3.2 Managing personal emotions and stress

The further up the management continuum one progresses, the more (many managers report) stress one is in danger of being put under. There is a myth that those in leadership positions should not show emotion. One of the causes of stress is the suppression of feelings. The competent supervisor does not suppress emotion but manages it. Decisions are made rationally and not in the heat of the moment. Personal likes and dislikes have no place in the decision-making process.

The competent supervisor/FLM does not take criticism as a personal affront but as an opportunity to learn more about the task, more about those around him or her and more about his or herself. Criticism is viewed as constructive and not destructive.

When others have problems, the competent supervisor/FLM supports but does not become so involved that he or she cannot be objective.

THINK POINT

How do you react to criticism: does it make you defensive? What do you do to handle stress and how do you relax?

Consider the following questions:

- Are you satisfied that your response demonstrates your personal competence?
- Can you control your levels of stress?
- Are you able to use your position to reduce stress in the work-place?
- Do you remain calm in difficult or uncertain situations?
- Do you give a constant and stable performance under pres-sure?
- Can you accept personal criticism without becoming defen-sive?
- Can you handle the emotions of others without becoming too involved?

Action Plan
What steps can you take to ensure that you 'manage your personal emotions and stress'?

3.3 Managing personal learning and development

Learning and development are on-going processes. By reading *In Charge* you have made a commitment to your own development. The competent supervisor/FLM is aware of his or her needs for training and development; they recognize their personal strengths and weaknesses and plan to play to the former and eliminate the latter.

Mistakes and problems are seen as learning opportunities and challenges to be overcome, and form part of a larger development plan that the competent supervisor has set for him or herself.

THINK POINT

Where will your learning and development go from here: is *In Charge* just a start to a process and not the end of it?

Consider the following questions:

- Are you satisfied that your response demonstrates your personal competence?
- Can you recognize and identify your own learning and development needs?
- What are you doing to meet your learning and development needs?
- Do you set challenges for yourself to develop your skills?
- Can you recognize your own strengths and weaknesses?
- Do you learn from your mistakes and the mistakes of others?
- Can you transfer learning from one situation to another?
- Can you adapt your behaviour as a result of feedback or new information?

Action Plan
What steps can you take to ensure that you 'manage your personal learning and development'?

This concludes *Managing People*, the first volume of *In Charge*. It is a starting point for considering the underpinning knowledge needed by the competent supervisor/FLM. It will not make you competent – no book can do that – but it has attempted to provide you with the knowledge needed to understand the Management Charter Initiative Standards for supervisors, and from that knowledge, considered in respect of your work situation, can flow competence.

References

Adair, J. (1983): *Effective Leadership*. London, Gower.

Ardrey, R. (1967): *The Territorial Imperative*. London, Collins.

Argyris, C. (1960): *Understanding Organizational Behaviour*. London, Tavistock Institute.

Asch, S. E. (1951): 'Effects of Group Pressure Upon the Modification and Distortion of Judgements'. In Guetzkow, *Leadership and Men*. New York, Carnegie Press.

Belbin, M. (1981): *Management Teams, Why They Succeed or Fail*. Oxford, Heinemann.

Bernstein, B. (1961): 'Social Structure, Language and Learning'. *Educational Research*, 3.

Blake, R. and Mouton, J. (1964): *The Managerial Grid*. New York, Gulf.

Buchanan, D. and Huczynski, H. (1985): *Organizational Behaviour*. London, Prentice Hall.

Cattell, R. (1951): 'New Concepts for Measuring Group Syntality'. *Human Relations*, 4.

Cole, G. (1988): *Personnel Management, Theory and Practice*. London, DP Publications.

Deutsch, M. (1949): 'A Theory of Cooperation and Competition'. *Human Relations*, 2.

Eyre, E. C. (1991): *Mastering Basic Management*. New York, Harper Collins.

Fayol, H. (1916): *General and Industrial Administration*. Translated from the French by C. Storrs (1949), London, Pitman.

Fiedler, F. (1964): *A Theory of Leadership Effectiveness*. New York, McGraw Hill.

Handy, C. (1976): *Understanding Organizations*. London, Penguin.

Handy, C. (1988): *Making Managers*. London, Pitman.

Handy, C. (1991): *The Gods of Management*, 3rd edn. London, Century Business Books.

Hastings, C., Bixby, P. and Chaudry-Lawton, R. (1986): *Superteams – A Blueprint for Organisational Success*. London, Gower.

Homans, G. (1950): *The Human Group*. New York, Harcourt Brace.

Honey, P. and Mumford, J. (1986): *A Manual of Learning Styles*. Maidenhead, P. Honey.

Janis, I. (1968): *Victims of Group Think – A Psychological Study of Foreign Policy Decisions and Fiascos*. Boston, Mass., Houghton Mifflin.

Kolb, D. et al. (1979): *Organizational Psychology: An Experiential Approach*. New Jersey, Prentice Hall.

Lawrence, P. and Lorsch, J. (1967): *Organizations and Environment*. Harvard, Harvard Business School.

Lloyd, S. (1988): *How to Develop Assertiveness*. London, Kogan Page.

Lorenz, K. (1963): *Zur Naturgeschichte der Aggression*. Translated (1966) as *On Aggression*. London, Methuen.

McClelland, D. C. (1961): *The Achieving Society*. New York, The Free Press.

McGregor, D. (1960): *The Human Side of Enterprise*. New York, McGraw Hill.

Margerison, C. J. and McCann, D. J. (1985): *How to Lead a Winning Team*. Bradford, University Press.

Morris, D. (1969): *The Human Zoo*. London, Jonathan Cape.

Peters, T. and Waterman, R. (1981): *In Search of Excellence*. New York, Harper and Row.

Pugh, D. (ed.) (1971): *Organizational Theory, Selected Readings*. Harmondsworth, Penguin.

Reddy, M. (1987): *The Manager's Guide to Counselling at Work*. Leicester, British Psychological Society.

Roger, A. (1952): *The Seven Point Plan*. London, NIIP.

Roethlisberger, F. J. and Dickson, W. J. (1964): *Management and the Worker*. New York, John Wiley and Sons.

Shaw, M. (1976): *Group Dynamics*. New York, McGraw Hill.

Schein, E. H. (1980): *Organizational Psychology*, 3rd edn. New Jersey, Prentice Hall.

Schein, E. H. (1984): 'Coming to a New Awareness of Organisational Culture'. *Sloan Management Review*.

Sherif, M. (1936): *The Social Psychology of Group Norms*. New York, Harper and Row.

Sherif, M. and Sherif, C. (1956): *An Outline of Social Psychology*. New York, McGraw Hill.

Tannenbaum, R. and Schmidt, W. (1973): 'How to Choose a Leadership Pattern'. *Harvard Business Review*, May/June.

Taylor, F. W. (1911): *Principles of Scientific Management*. New York, Harper.

Tice, L. (1989): *Investment in Excellence* (Multi Media). Seattle, Pacific Institute.

Urwick, L. (1947): *The Elements of Administration*. London, Pitman.

Whetton, D. and Cameron, K. (1982): *Developing Management Skills*. Basingstoke, Macmillan.

Woodward, J. (1958): *Industrial Organization and Practice*. Oxford, University Press.

Yablonsky, L. (1964): *The Violent Gang*. New York, Macmillan.

Index